FRONTIERS
OF
HEAVEN

FRONTIERS
OF
HEAVEN

A Journey to the End of China

STANLEY STEWART

THE LYONS PRESS
Guilford, Connecticut
An imprint of The Globe Pequot Press

For my mother and father, with love and admiration

The Lyons Press is an imprint of The Globe Pequot Press.

Originally published by Flamingo, an imprint of HarperCollins UK

10 9 8 7 6 5 4 3 2 1

Printed in the United States of America

Map by Stefanie Ward

Library of Congress Cataloging-in-Publication Data
Stewart, Stanley, 1952—
        Frontiers of heaven : a journey to the end of China / Stanley Stewart.
            p. cm.
        Originally published : London, Murray, 1995.
        ISBN 1-59228-401-9
1. Stewart, Stanley, 1952- —Travel—China. 2. China—Description and travel. I.
Title: Journey to the end of China. II. Title
DS712.S77 2004
915.104′59—dc22
                                                                        2004046460

ACKNOWLEDGMENTS

If a writer's life is solitary, a traveller's is not. The milestones of journeys are the people you meet, and I was blessed in China and in Pakistan with many happy encounters. Throughout the book I have changed people's names to protect their privacy, and to guard them against political criticism should more severe times return to China. I am grateful for their hospitality, their tolerance, and their insights. I hope they will forgive me for the presumption of marching through their lives and them writing about them.

The completion of this book was made possible by a grant from the Author's Foundation. The final text has gained much from the scrutiny and wise advice of Grant McIntyre, Gail Pirkis and Liz Robinson. Throughout, my parents have offered support and encouragement and I dedicate the result to them.

Contents

ILLUSTRATIONS

(between pages 116 and 117)

All photographs were taken by the author.

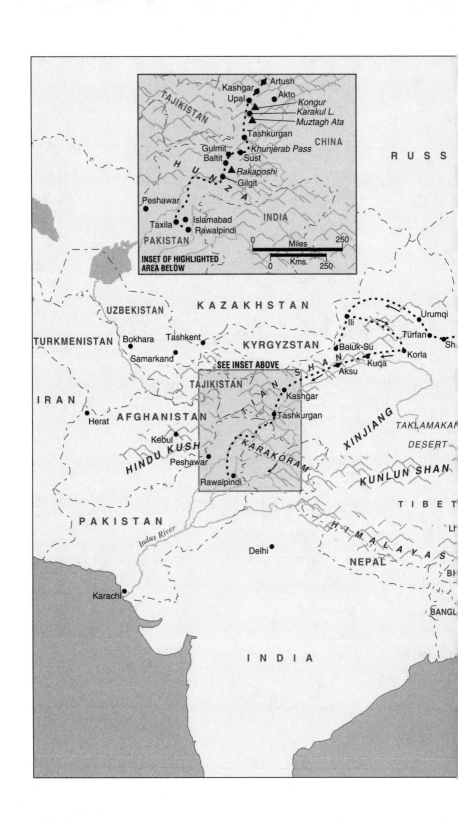

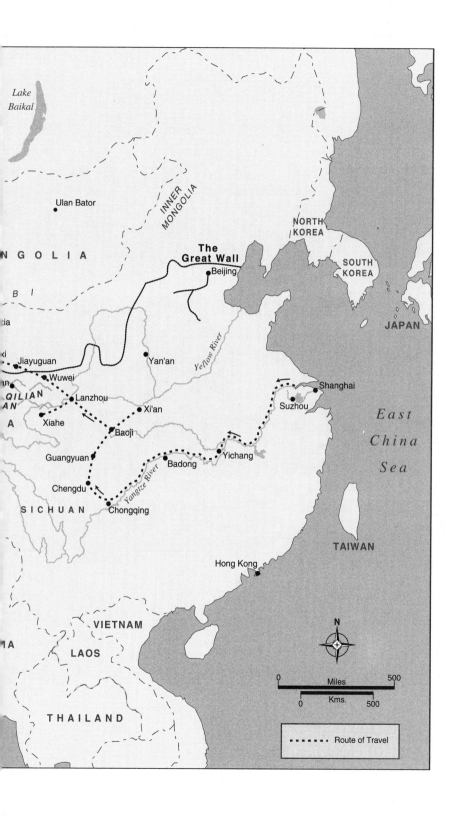

One

DANCING ON THE BUND

I first saw him on the Bund in Shanghai, dancing in a long corridor of sun, his arm around an imaginary partner.

He was an old man fluttering amongst sedate couples, his head inclined slightly as if his invisible partner was murmuring in his ear. He danced the two-step. So elegant was he, with his feet skating, it was a moment before I noticed he had only one arm. The left sleeve of his jacket was empty, fastened to the pocket with a safety-pin.

The old man was one of those who gathered in the gardens of the Bund every morning to dance to the tunes of a bygone age played on someone's cassette player. They came from all over Shanghai on their bicycles. At this early hour the promenade was full of people limbering up for the day. The ballroom dancing shared the morning with *tai chi*, calisthenics, and a mysterious exercise performed by three old women in a flower bed rubbing their backs on the trunks of the camphor trees.

Among the dancers many of the men were old enough to remember the heyday of ballroom dancing. "Begin the Beguine" and "Sentimental Journey" were the songs of their youth. The women they partnered through grave foxtrots tended to be younger, escaping into fantasy rather than memory. The early light stretched their entwined shadows far out into the road where they flickered through the hot traffic. Above them the grand old buildings of the Bund, built in the era of these dance tunes, were moored along the waterfront, like liners with their bows turned to the river and the morning sun.

Unexpectedly the dancing broke up with the threat of fisticuffs, as in a rowdy nightclub. A party of elderly women performing *tai chi* exercises with long ceremonial swords began to encroach upon the dancers' space as their numbers swelled. A territorial battle of wills was joined as the two groups circled ever nearer. When a frail octogenarian nearly decapitated a waltzing couple, tempers flared and passers-by struggled to keep the elderly protagonists apart.

The fracas signaled the end of the morning rituals, and the dancers began to drift away to their bicycles and their jobs. When I looked around I found the one-armed man at my side. He smiled at me as if we knew each other. His face was crinkled with age. He introduced himself.

"My name is Wang," he said, "and I am ninety-nine years of age."

I had come to China on the Trans–Siberian Express from Moscow, leaving Yaroslavl station at midnight with my compartment full of moonlight, and champagne at a dollar a bottle. For a week I had rattled across landscapes of birch trees and cold lakes and muddy villages floating amid cabbages. The scale of Siberia was breathtaking. Roads ran for hundreds of miles without any sign of traffic. Horizons seemed to be countries away. Clouds as big as Kent sailed between distant mountains.

From the shores of Lake Baikal, the line cut south across the endless undulating pasture of Mongolia. Here and there encampments of white yurts and parties of horsemen broke the empty horizons. Mongolia felt like a vacant lot, given over to grass and weeds, standing on the edge of the world.

But these steppes lie at the centre of Asia's history. This is the continent's great grassy heart, whose nomadic inhabitants have troubled all the civilizations that lie around its rim, from China to India to the Mediterranean and on to Muscovy. This emptiness, and the careless untamed people who live here, have been China's great terror since its earliest days. The Great Wall, the only man-made object visible from space, was built to keep that terror at bay.

China arrived one morning before breakfast. I opened the blinds to find a landscape of dense cultivation, the antithesis of Mongolia. Peasants in lampshade hats stood calf deep in rice paddies. An old man drove an ox-cart along a dusty lane between lines of poplars to a village lapped round with crops. It was a garden landscape where every tree was a planted tree and every inch of land was tamed. The mountains in the distance were the mountains of Chinese painting, the colour running slightly in their flanks. Curtains of mist were draped between the trees.

At Qinglongqiao the train passed beneath the Great Wall. An hour later I was in Beijing. A week later I took the train to Shanghai on China's eastern seaboard where I was ready to begin my journey. It was to be a journey out of China. I wanted to cross the country to the very end of the Great Wall, almost 2,000 miles away. There I wanted to step "beyond the mouth," as the Chinese say. My destination was Xinjiang in the northwest, a fearful region of desert and mountains and unpredictable people, the outer darkness beyond the Celestial Kingdom, inhabited by the barbarians of Chinese legend.

The road to the north-west was the Silk Road, the mother of all trade routes, which had brought caravans to China in search of luxury and exotica. For western merchants it had been a path to riches. For the Chinese, the road has more complex associations. The regions beyond the wall exercise an ambivalent fascination. They know the Silk Road as the Journey to the West, an odyssey that has become a moral fable.

For the Chinese, the road began as a promise. In the end it promised only exile.

I had arranged to meet Wang two days later for lunch in the guest dining-room of the Jade Buddha Temple. In the court yards the monks floated through clouds of incense like heavy brown birds. I had spent much of the morning looking over the halls with their apoplectic guardians and smug Buddhas. The temple's great treasure is a six-foot Buddha carved out of a single piece of white jade. He resides in an upstairs library lined with wooden cases containing the sutras brought from India along the Silk Road a millennium ago.

One approached shoeless under the disapproving gaze of an elderly monk. The Buddha was a demure effeminate creature with a smile that made the Mona Lisa look gauche. Coolly detached, he seemed unsympathetic, as if the unhappiness of the world was an irrelevance. Here lies a great difference of temperament. Christ is a figure of suffering; he is telling us he understands, and his understanding makes him sympathetic. The Buddha is a figure of transcendence. He makes our suffering look foolish; he is telling us it is unnecessary. He does not indulge us with the sympathy that is the currency of a kinder and less mature society.

His elegant aloof face captured my first impression of the Chinese: indifference. That they should be indifferent to me was understandable, but they seemed equally indifferent to each other. It was a flawed impression, formed in ignorance in the first confused weeks, but five months later it would still nag at me.

I found Wang waiting in the dining-room. It was like a restaurant in a Chinese hotel: linen table-cloths, shoals of bored waitresses, tanks of unhappy fish.

"Are you a Buddhist?" Wang asked, as we took our seats.

"No," I said. "I'm just looking."

"I'm not a Buddhist either," he said. "But the food is very good. Look." He held up the menu. "No meat, of course. But you can have a choice of whisky or cognac with your meal. The monks have become so . . ."—he searched a moment—"eager to please."

The old man had aged beautifully. His skin was as delicate as rice paper. He moved slowly but lightly as if life had taught him care. For a moment I gazed at him as one might examine an artefact: a hundred-year-old man.

I asked him what he did. He had been very particular about the time of our lunch as if his days were busy.

"I am a money-changer, and a guide. Perhaps I can be of assistance to you. Do you have American dollars?" The city was full of money-changers. The rates were good; Shanghai's hunger for foreign currency seemed insatiable.

"One or two hotels know me," the old man went on. "Sometimes I act as a guide for foreigners looking for old Shanghai. The houses they grew up in. The houses of parents and grandparents."

"You must know Shanghai well."

"It is my home. I know many Shanghais."

"Which is the best?"

He shrugged. "The first Shanghai. The first memories. Like the first girl. This is always the best."

His life had a breathless quality. His father had been a *comprador,* a Chinese agent for one of the large foreign firms that already dominated Shanghai by the end of the last century. The family had been wealthy and between the wars Wang had been a part of the cosmopolitan life of the city to which few Chinese had access. He spoke English and French. He was a regular at the races and frequented the dance-halls of the French Concession. Living off his father's money, he dabbled in antiques, had a stint as a minor film actor, and ran a dancing studio. This was his "first" Shanghai, the city of the Twenties when his life had been carefree.

A waitress brought the meal, an armful of dishes. The old man's hands, pointing out the specialties, were mottled with age.

"I was a man-about-town." His English seemed to belong to another era. "Shanghai was so charming in those days. Everything seemed new. Everywhere full of excitements."

In 1928 Wang had married Ivana, one of the thousands of White Russian refugees who fled to Shanghai after the Russian Revolution. He had met her at Maxim's, a cabaret. It was a marriage made in hell.

"She was so beautiful," Wang said, screwing his eyes shut, conjuring a face young more than sixty years ago. "I think at first I must have been very much in love with her. I felt sorry for her too. She was so far from home. She did not know if her family were alive. She was an exile here. Vulnerability is so seductive."

"What happened?"

"She found someone who could protect her better than I. Women are survivors. It is the men who are the romantics. She ran away to Australia with a shipping broker." I must have looked concerned. "After a long time the ashes go cold. Your life ceases to belong to you and becomes just another story."

Through the Thirties Wang's fortunes had declined as he squandered what was left of his inheritance. He had owned a club in Fuzhou Lu and lost it to pay gambling debts. He had worked for Sir Victor Sassoon, and been on the payroll of the gangster Big-Eared Du. In those days, Du was the unofficial mayor of Shanghai. Half the city seemed to work for him.

When the Communists came to power, Wang had undergone political re-education, then worked through the Fifties as a night-watchman. Life had not prepared him for a world without influence and money. But he was resigned, even content.

"It was not such a bad time," he said. "I was not a young man anymore. I felt sorry for younger people who were missing the excitements, the opportunities. For me there was something like relief. Shanghai had been too crazy. Communism was the asylum."

The Cultural Revolution that swept through China in 1966 had been his undoing. Wang proved an obvious target for the Red Guards. When they searched his apartment they found foreign books, letters from foreigners, a collection of old coins, a marriage certificate to a Russian wife, paintings that had belonged to his grandfather—a veritable treasure-trove of seditious material. The Red Guards, some of them as young as sixteen, paraded him through the streets, a poster round his neck declaring his counter-revolutionary crimes. At a public rally, he was beaten for lack of enthusiasm in his self-criticism. Eventually he was shipped to a labour camp in Xinjiang, beyond the Great Wall.

Wang believed it was not so much his bourgeois past as his association with Jiang Qing, the Shanghai film actress who had married Chairman Mao, that was his undoing. Madam Mao used the Cultural Revolution to obscure her own past and to settle old scores. Anyone who had known her before her marriage to Mao was in danger. Wang was only one name on a very long list of former associates who suffered.

"Do you remember her?" I asked. "From her days as a film actress? What was she like?"

He shook his head. "I don't remember her. That is the strange thing. She was one of a circle of people around the film studios in those days. I must have met her. But I can't remember her. So many times in Xinjiang, I tried to remember."

It was a terrible vision, the old man packed into a freightcar with hundreds of others, sifting his memories for the woman who had done this to him. Would it have been any easier if he had found her, a pale moon of a face floating up out of the past, a young woman laughing at a party, perhaps, being introduced by a friend, meeting his eye?"

What did you do in Xinjiang?"

"I worked in a mine near Tulufan. Ten years in the desert. In the summers it was a furnace. In the winters we had frostbite. It was hell. There were many suicides." He picked absent-mindedly at the food. "I lost my arm there. There was an accident with one of the conveyor belts. After that life was easier because I worked in the office."

I felt guilty asking about these terrible times. My curiosity had turned the lunch sour.

"But I talk too much of myself," he said. "It is the failing of old people. Tell me about yourself. You have only just come to China, I think. But where are you going?"

I told him I was going to Xinjiang. He chuckled at the irony of this.

"What is there to see?" he cried. "A wasteland. And unhappy people. From Shanghai to Xinjiang. You are going in the wrong direction. Shanghai is a destination, not Xinjiang."

I told him I would follow the Silk Road.

He mopped his chin with a napkin. "I have something to show you. Come."

He vanished down a flight of steps into the courtyard where I found him, wreathed in incense, pointing at the roof.

Set along the ridge-tiles of a temple was a stone carving. A horseman was emerging from a fortress gate into a fairy-tale landscape of pointed hills and contorted pines. He was accompanied by a monkey, a madman and a servant.

"The Journey to the West," the old man said. "Your journey.'

The carvings represented the pilgrimage of Xuan Zhang along the Silk Road to the Buddhist shrines of India. Or rather, it represented the legend that had grown from this journey, with its four emblematic characters, struggling against the vicissitudes of outlandish fate. It was a pilgrimage, a quest, a rite of passage and a tall tale, all elevated on this temple roof into a religious icon: the journey as revelation and as salvation. It sounded promising.

I fell in love with Shanghai. It was an impossible city, teeming, filthy, rapacious. The hotels were overcrowded and the streets were full of hustlers. In June the heat was already unbearable and the stench of Suzhou Creek crept along the deep avenues, a malodorous public health warning.

I loved the extravagance of its past and the tawdry echoes of it to be found on every corner. Roaming through Shanghai was like rooting through the effects of a great-aunt whose life has long been the scandal of the family. We may not have approved, but we are fascinated and charmed. She was a glamorous figure in a more glamorous world.

Europeans invented Shanghai. The Treaty of Nanking signed aboard a British warship in 1842 established it as a concessionary port where foreign traders could operate independently of Chinese customs and laws. The long decades of extra-territoriality created a colonial cosmopolitan city which entertained the illusion that it was immune to the country of which it was a part.

In the hothouse climate of the Orient, Shanghai was a bit of Europe grown grotesque. Wedged between the East China Sea and a thousand miles of rice paddies, the splendid façade of the Bund, its neo-classical and art deco buildings which still greet ships sailing up the Huangpu, owes nothing to China, except cheap labour. In Shanghai's glory days, between the two world wars, you could order a well-cut suit, a French dinner, the latest automobile, or a set of monogrammed golf clubs. You could watch horse-races, baseball games, or football matches. You could attend the opera, take in a theatre matinée or visit the club to play billiards, bowls or bridge. You could conduct business spanning three continents and gossip in five languages. In Shanghai's climate of excess, there was never any shortage of gossip. "One never asked why someone came to Shanghai," Lady Jellicoe warned. "It was assumed that everyone had something to hide."

The missionaries who came hunting Chinese souls declared that if God allowed Shanghai to survive, then he owed an apology to Sodom and Gomorrah. In a city where Mammon was God, only the pursuit of pleasure rivaled the pursuit of money. Shanghai was called the whore of the East, and it catered for every taste. Gambling clubs, race-tracks, dancehalls, opium dens, freak shows and music halls all vied with each other for trade. "If you want girls, or boys, you can have them, at all prices," Christopher Isherwood wrote. "If you want opium you can smoke it in the best company, served on a tray like afternoon tea." Evenings that began at the famous and entirely respectable Long Bar in the Shanghai Club had a way of degenerating through cabarets and brothels to the gin shops of Blood Alley. Finally, should you wish to repent, there were churches and chapels of every denomination.

Inevitably there was another side to this story. The American journalist Edgar Snow, who came to Shanghai in the late Twenties, described the terrible conditions of child slave labourers, sold into factories before the age of ten and unable to leave the walled and guarded premises without a special permit. Poverty in the Chinese city was horrific; for every Chinese like Wang enjoying a life of privilege, there were thousands consigned to the misery of fetid slums. When the last revellers made their way home along the Avenue Edward VII, dinner-jackets askew, they passed trucks on their morning rounds collecting the night's harvest of corpses.

Like a stage set whose cast has departed, the grand buildings of old Shanghai remain, engulfed now by the pervasive crowds of all Chinese cities, tides of cyclists and waves of slippered feet, incongruous against the classical façades. Broken into tenements and adorned with laundry, their ornate balconies overflow with potted plants, bird cages, and upturned bicycles. In the manner of re-educated capitalists, many have been assigned new jobs. The British Consulate, set behind lawns made for croquet, has become an institute for international studies. The Jardine Matheson building has found work as a state textile firm. The Hong Kong and Shanghai Bank, where British lions once stood guard, is now a municipal office guarded by soldiers in cotton slippers.

At the end of the Bund is the Shanghai Club, once so exclusive that the doorman was obliged to consult members before admitting passers-by caught in the cross-fire of a gun battle in the street. The Club is now a seamen's hostel where Malaysian soldiers, broad as tree trunks, argue over their diminutive Chinese girlfriends. In the Gents the porcelain bears the hallmark Doulton & Co, Lambeth, London. The snooker room across the hall seems to have been forgotten. For a moment you could be in St James's. Everything is as it was sixty years ago, except the height of the tables. When the Japanese occupied the city, they had the legs cut down to improve their cue action.

Wang and I became great companions, and during the fortnight I spent in Shanghai we saw a good deal of each other. He was the embodiment of the city I longed to know. I was someone who never grew tired of his stories.

We had dinner together and went to the opera. He took me to the museum to look at the bronzes and the Tang dynasty horses and to tea in the Huxinting tea-house where opium used to be served with the sweets. We took the cruise boat out to the mouth of the Yangtze where the sea shone beneath a bright dome of haze. In the glare the horizon had vanished. We seemed to have reached world's end, a still, calm place of blinding light.

On our jaunts about the city, he populated the streets with ghosts from the past. On the Bund he told me about Chiang Kai-shek's soldiers, on the eve of the Communist entry into the city, carrying the gold bullion out of the banks in the glare of headlights and loading them onto ships bound for Taiwan. In Renmin park he conjured the old racecourse with its thoroughbreds, its ladies with parasols, and its touts in black pyjamas and brown trilbys. In the Nanjing Road he described the decorated rickshaws of the sing-song girls, their bells ringing as they went from one dinner engagement to another. Passing the old Astor Hotel one day, he took me into the ballroom and showed me the corner where he had been sitting half a century before when a bellboy brought him a telegram with news of his wife's flight to Australia.

I joined him for lunch one day in one of the streets running off the Bund, a cool canyon between stone façades. We went up a broad stairway to the second floor where an elderly couple ran a lunch counter in the corridor, three tables pushed against the walls and an array of simmering pots in what had been a concierge's room. The old lady greeted Wang with a series of matronly clucks. Her husband smiled toothlessly from a doorway.

The building had been one of the grander apartment blocks and its ruin was compelling. The ground floor was now occupied by shoddy offices while the high-ceilinged apartments were broken up into one-roomed tenements. The corridors were crowded with old cupboards, bicycles, and junk. Electricity meters and clumps of wiring hung from the cornices. Above my head a pipe ran through a fanlight. Tenants had driven nails into the pilasters for coat-hooks. The grilled lift cage had grown cobwebs. People came and went, opening and closing doors of such grand proportions that a horseman could have ridden through them. Beyond, one glimpsed French windows and wrought-iron balconies cluttered with bird cages and old bedsteads. In the pediments above the doors, the swags of stone fruit were spattered with bird droppings.

The old woman brought a stew with pieces of pork like flattened footballs, a dish of soggy tofu and bowls of cold rice. It looked like Chinese school dinners. Wang wriggled his eyebrows and opened the beer.

"She is my niece," Wang said. "her grandmother is my mother." These old people, stooped and shuffling, were a generation younger than Wang. He fished a football from the murky depths. "Delicious. The taste of my childhood."

The sound of a quarrel echoed down the stairway from an upper floor.

"Do you know John McCormack?" Wang asked.

"The tenor?"

He nodded.

"McCormack is the sound of *my* childhood," I said.

Wang shook his head. "You are too young."

"It's true," I protested. "I used to listen to his records at my grandparents. In Ireland. He was an Irish tenor."

McCormack was of the generation that succeeded Caruso. Purists never forgave him for wasting his talent on Irish folk songs. But as I boy I had been entranced by them, distant crackling recordings made before the First War. The sad Irish melodies seemed to float up from some deep well of the past. They were the perfect echo of Irish exile. I could still sing them all.

"Oh Kathleen Mavoureen, my sad tears are falling
To think that from Erin and from thee I must part.
It may be for years or it may be forever—
Oh why art thou silent, the voice of my heart."

"Bravo," Wang laughed. He put his chopsticks down and clapped. The old woman came round the corner and stared. Then, seizing on the opportunity to translate this good humour into a sale, she fetched another bottle of beer.

"He was here in Shanghai," Wang said. "In '32 or '33 I think, for a season at the Grand Theatre."

"John McCormack was in Shanghai?"

"Upstairs," Wang said through a mouthful of rice. "He lived upstairs. The producer lent him his apartment."

I tried to picture him in the corridor, a burly figure in a tweed suit and spats, but the image was dispelled by a man shuffling past in a bathrobe and plastic sandals.

"They were the songs of home," I said.

The old man looked at me with new curiosity. We had talked so much about Shanghai, he had almost come to assume that I was part of the old expatriate community. He seemed to realize suddenly that I was a stranger, that he knew nothing about me.

"Where is home?" he asked.

"I'm not sure," I said.

"Ireland is not home?"

"Yes, I suppose. But I left when I was a boy."

He was intrigued, and had momentarily forgotten the pork footballs.

"But where do you belong?" he asked.

"I don't *belong* anywhere."

He seemed startled by this rootlessness. His own life was so much the creation of a place, of Shanghai.

"Yours is a life of departures." He waved his chopsticks at me as if he had solved a riddle. "This is why you have come to Shanghai."

Two

A RHINOCEROS LOOKING AT THE MOON

To the Chinese it is *Chang Jiang,* the Great River. It runs through the nation's consciousness like some profound, if elusive, idea. Poets called it the River of Heaven and painters spent whole careers trying to capture its soul. In innumerable legends it is not so much a setting as a character, mysterious, treacherous, divine. When it broke its banks, emperors were perceived to have lost the Mandate of Heaven and dynasties fell. When Li Bai, China's most popular poet, drowned in the river in the eighth century while trying to embrace a reflection of the moon, he seemed to symbolize a national obsession.

After the Amazon and the Nile, the Yangtze is the longest river in the world. Rising, like so many of the great rivers of Asia, among the glaciers of Tibet, it runs almost four thousand miles to the sea, across ten provinces, each as big as a country. Joined by 700 tributaries, it drains an area of half a million square miles, ten times the size of England. The Chinese say if you haven't been up the Great River you haven't been anywhere.

Passenger boats ply the Yangtze as far as Chongqing, 1,500 miles upstream. In a way I would come to recognize in China, people spoke of tickets in the despairing tones that one might speak of Centre Court seats at Wimbledon. Tickets of any sort were China's Holy Grail. I was rescued by old Shanghai. Wang secured me a cabin on a boat to Chongqing with a judicious mix of contacts, bribes, and the exchange of favours. I confess to having enjoyed this whiff of corruption.

The elation of travel becomes an addiction. The familiar rush of euphoria at the prospect of departure feeds some appetite for innocence. On the Bund with my ticket, the Huangpu full of boats and sunlight, I felt twelve years old again. The sensation of freedom made me light on my feet. I was embarking on a journey upriver as a prelude to a journey that would take me half-way across Asia, to the Gobi desert, the oases of the Taklamakan, the high passes of the Pamirs. I felt like Mole skipping out of his burrow in *The Wind in the Willow*. The morning smelt of wonderful adventures, new landscapes, and the unexpected. Anything could happen, and much of it would. The moment of departure is the closest one comes to recreating the delicious anticipations of childhood.

The journey upriver was to take a week. I boarded the night before sailing. Shanghai was falling asleep, its lighted windows nodding off one by one. The sad old faces of the buildings of the Bund were in darkness. In the gardens, where the dancers would be arriving in a few hours, young couples who had nowhere else to meet were entwined on the stone benches, while along the sea wall vagrant Uighur lads from Xinjiang were settling down for the night.

On the boat I wandered the empty gangways for some time before finding an attendant who showed me to my cabin. It was perfect—a high-sided bunk, a sink, a small dresser, a chair, all pleasingly nautical. Through the open door I looked down on the quay: gas-lit stalls selling biscuits, nuts and watermelons, and a group of boatmen playing pool. I fell asleep over maps. The sound of the clicking balls, the murmur of commerce and the slap of the river crept into my dreams like stowaways.

In the morning I woke to the sound of sobbing and went out to find a girl clinging to a sailor at the rail below. The quay had been overtaken by the anxious theatrics of departure. A stream of coolies clambered up the gangway under vast sacks. Families bobbed back and forth, ferrying baggage and children. The crowds eddying around the sailor and the girl were heedless of her breaking heart. Plump and adolescent, she sobbed on his shoulder, her eyes a blur of mascara. Had the oblivious crowds paused to look, they would have been shocked by this unseemly display: the black mini-skirt, the high heels, the make-up, the public tears. She was alone with her grief. Her sailor lounged against the rail like another spectator.

We winched off the quay on our own anchor chain. In mid stream the engines started and the boat shuddered. The girl stood apart from the waving throng, her hand clamped pathetically over her mouth. At a distance she looked like the child she was. Her sailor had vanished into the ship's crowds, eager to unpack.

Where the Huangpu meets the Yangtze, the parent river is twelve miles wide. With the East China Sea almost in sight, the Great River seems to have lost all interest in its destination. Fat and sluggish, a creature of tides as much as of currents, the river seems possessed of a rather sinister ennui as if, after a long and eventful journey, it has grown wary of arrival.

For its last thousand miles, from Yichang to the coast, the lower Yangtze maintains this lazy indifference. It crosses the great rice plains of East China, falling barely an inch a mile. The serenity of this wide slow stream belies the violence that it has regularly unleashed on these vulnerable lowlands. It is the prerogative of rivers, who have brought life to those along their banks, to threaten all they have created, a prerogative the Yangtze regularly exercises. The floods in the eastern plains sound like a knell through China's history.

Rivers can be strangely immune to their own banks. For three days we sailed upstream on a silver panorama of water oblivious of the most recent floods. From the decks we could see that the river had broken its banks. The waters appeared to have flooded inland as far as a line of dykes. In drowned orchards men rowed skiffs in the watery lanes. Gulls wheeled over flooded fields of maize looking for fish, and local steamers were moored against houses where the river lapped the window sills. They were picturesque images, devoid of distress.

But the truth, which we only learned on arrival in Chongqing, was that this was not minor local flooding but a national disaster. The river had breached the dykes and a great swathe of eastern China was under water. Countless hectares of crops were lost and millions of people had been made homeless. The army had been mobilized, international aid was arriving, and the death toll had risen to 2,500. The world was watching scenes of sodden refugees whose houses were melting like biscuits. Afloat on the belly of the culprit, I saw only trees knee-deep in their own reflections and ducks paddling contentedly among water-logged haystacks.

Between these flooded banks, the life of the river went on undisturbed. Rust-stained freighters made their way upstream to Nanking. Local ferries and tramp steamers hustled between the endless trains of barges heaped with gravel and cement and bamboo. Under the awnings of sampans drifting beneath our bows whole families were at dinner in a flurry of chopsticks. Fishing boats threw splayed nets that stood like giant spiders in the current. In this traffic the passenger ships of The East is Red Line, the aristocrats of the river, hooted at each other like trains as they passed, signaling distant destinations.

In Communist China first class was abolished as a concession to egalitarianism. This did little to inhibit the country's natural inclination to hierarchical distinction. On The East is Red No. 57, there were five main classes with further innumerable subdivisions. Top of the pile were the second class staterooms, where I was accommodated in an outside cabin. Behind frosted glass doors, they were a world apart—carpeted, erratically air-conditioned, and provided with western-style toilets, showers, and a sun lounge in the bow furnished like a dentist's waiting room.

Amidships was third class: shared cabins with the subdivision of four, six or eight bunks. On the lower decks was fourth class: dormitory accommodation with ranks of steel bunks bolted to the walls. An unofficial fifth class occupied the corridors, stairwells and gangways, where people camped on the metal floors like refugees, separated from each other and from the boat's rising tide of litter by low walls of their meagre belongings.

Second class was the usual mix of party cadres, industrial managers, and Overseas Chinese from Singapore, Malaysia and Hong Kong. Others were more mysterious. A couple of cabins away were two putative starlets, fresh from a fortnight of auditions in the Shanghai film studios, now on their way home, full of cosmopolitan airs.

Round on the starboard side, No. 4 cabin was occupied by one of the delightful old women in which China seems to specialize: serene, angelic, and street-wise, an oriental Miss Marple. In the mornings she did her *tai chi* on the bow deck, a slow-motion figure in a veil of grey mist. She had a suitor, a mischievous elderly gentleman who came calling on her bearing gifts of oranges. They sat in her cabin giggling together like children. In the evenings they were the stars of the dance floor with a silky waltz.

In the bow the sun lounge had been turned into a cross between a dormitory and a gaming house. The armchairs had been pushed together and made into communal day beds. The plastic plants had been hung with laundry. The television console had been seconded as a drinks trolley, and at tables all round the room gamblers were huddled over card games.

Gambling has long been a national obsession of the Chinese. In the old days housewives could hardly buy vegetables without shooting craps with the greengrocer, double or quits. The Communists declared gambling illegal but succeeded in suppressing it only temporarily. Now, with less puritanical official attitudes, it is bubbling to the surface again. The lounge of The East is Red No. 57 would have done justice to any Mississippi riverboat. The tension was terrific. The players slapped down their cards and barked at each other through thick clouds of smoke. Family fortunes appeared to hang in the balance, and losers invariably left the room in tears.

I had become friends with the sailor whose departure had caused such grief on the quay at Shanghai. He made frequent excursions from third class to discuss Tang poetry with me. He was a cadet in the Chinese navy, going home to Chongqing on leave before his first posting. Far from the swaggering heart-breaker one might have expected, he was a thin nervous boy whose civilian clothes, like the white uniform, make him look like a man auditioning for a part. He had chosen to travel by boat instead of by train for romantic reasons. He was devoted to the poet Li Bai. The river journey was like a visit to the grave.

"He was drunk," the sailor said, explaining the fall into the river. "He was very inspiring when he was drunk. He was a traveler like you. Always wandering, without family, without a home." He made travelling sound like part of a larger tragedy.

Li Bai's iconoclastic reputation, common enough for western poets, is more unusual in China. He satirized Confucian traditions and shocked oriental sensibilities with a scandalous private life. Most disturbing to his contemporaries was his refusal to sit for the official examinations that would allow him entrance to the élite of the civil service. It was thought both selfish and naïve for a talented man not to spend a part of his career at the service of the Empire and the people.

His talent, however, was never in dispute. In his own lifetime Li Bai's work inspired adulation. He composed at breathtaking speed, particularly when drunk. Those who met him spoke of his piercing eyes and his compelling voice. Charismatic and disdainful, he was numbered among the "fallen immortals." His verses are full of dream journeys, of the loneliness of departure and exile, of the thrill of new worlds. It is the poetry of metaphorical travel. His demise in the waters of the Yangtze, which runs through Chinese literature as a moon-filled symbol of transience and renewal, seems almost to spring from his own imagery.

The sailor called round regularly to recite verses about the Yangtze from a book of poetry. He performed in the gangway outside my cabin with the gestures of a second-rate Olivier.

"After sudden rain, a clear autumn night . . .
The river of Heaven, white from eternity
The Yangtze's shallows limpid . . ."

The starlets, loitering in the doorway of their cabin, now wandered up the gangway. I had been musing on the collective noun for them, and had decided on a swank of starlets.

"Why are you reading to this foreigner?" they asked.

"He is interested," the boy protested. "He is reading Li Bai and Du Fu in English." The two starlets looked in at me. I was lying on my bunk. They were stylish in polyester blouses and pleated skirts. They wore scarlet lipstick and baroque eyelashes. One had produced an immaculate kiss-curl across her forehead. They were enameled, indifferent, and disturbingly erotic.

"Where is he from?" one asked, gazing about my cabin as if it was an exhibit, taking in the maps, the books, the socks soaking in the sink.

"From England," the sailor said proudly, as if he was in some way responsible. "He is travelling to the west."

"Is he alone?" Their eyes scanned the cabin for evidence of a companion.

"*Dandu,*" the sailor intoned. Alone. Having scoured the cabin, the blank twinned gaze of the starlets settled on me. Under their shameless scrutiny, I began to feel like what they saw: a foreigner, peculiar looking, ridiculously tall, with a big nose and big feet, a person of incomprehensible motives, a person without connections or history, a person without a context. *Dandu.*

Above Yichang the Yangtze is a different creature. The broad languid stream gives way suddenly to a turbulent river which cuts down from the highlands of Sichuan through the Hubei Mountains in a series of thrilling gorges. It is these gorges which have made the Yangtze famous; they rank among the most spectacular river scenery in the world.

In the course of a morning the river turned from a world of horizontals to one of verticals. We passed between portal cliffs into canyons whose walls rose from the water to peaks, wreathed in clouds, two thousand feet above us. In this confinement the currents are fierce and unpredictable, running at over twenty knots in places. The river captains speak of this Yangtze as the enemy, and of its navigation as a kind of warfare.

Rain filled the gorges and ran in streams down the gangway of the boat. The sky had settled into the tree-tops and mountains floated in and out of view, ethereal among the clouds. Men carrying baskets on their backs climbed greasy paths between sheets of rock and fields of bedraggled maize.

Wherever soil had settled, so had a farmer. Half-timbered cottages barnacled the high slopes, their fields so steep that the farmers had to lower themselves into their crops like mountaineers. On the wooden porches, toddlers were tied to posts for safety. Streams of water poured from the high fields directly into the river below, where sampans were moored beneath the cliffs. Clouds curled up the ravines and became entangled in groves of shaggy trees. A bay opened in the cliffs revealing a junk at anchor, its rigging limp in the rain. The river itself was a cauldron of sinister whirlpools and white water. The rocks which reared on all sides echoed this agitation, breaking from the water in splintered and contorted formation, rising suddenly to massive headlands, bizarre pinnacles, and slate-coloured peaks. For the passengers gathered at the rails beneath umbrellas, it was almost too much. The Chinese are the world's greatest petrophiles. They plant stones were others might choose an herbaceous border. In landscapes their attention is compelled, not by trees or distant figures, but by granite and limestone. The more bizarre the shape, the more it pleases the Chinese eye. The Yangtze gorges are the petrophile's ultimate fantasy. All about me the Chinese panted and swooned.

On the Yangtze every gorge, every defile, and every rock has been lovingly named. I asked a member of the crew who patiently identified rocks as I pointed them out: Tear-drop No. 1, Pearl No. 7, The Weeping Lady, the Emperor's Guard. We passed through Yellow Cat Gorge, Ox Liver and Horse Lung Gorge, Military Books and Precious Sword Gorge, each name a story. In Lantern Shadow Gorge a line of four spectacular peaks trailing long scarves of cloud represented the characters of the Journey to the West: the pilgrim Xuan Zang standing on the edge of a precipice, his faithful companion, Monkey, peering into the distance, Sandy carrying the luggage, and Pigsy riding a horse. On and on they went: Iron Coffin Rock, Dragon Door Gorge, Hanging Monk Rock. My favourite was Rhinoceros Looking at the Moon, a huge stone teetering uncertainly atop a black cliff, gazing mournfully at the sinking moon. The stories were full of floods and earthquakes, jade dragons and sacred oxen, old kings, armoured warriors and virtuous maidens. Everyone came and went on clouds, and was on a first-name basis with the Immortals. This fearful river underpinned a world of reassuring fictions where good triumphed over evil, and order over chaos.

The river's reality was rather darker. A lesser people might have declared the Yangtze gorges unnavigable; it is a measure of Chinese will and genius that they did not. The battle was won, however, at considerable cost. In Kongling Tang rapids alone, seventeen steamships went down between 1900 and 1945; the deadliest of its rocks, now dynamited, was known as "Come to Me." Above the Xin Tang rapids stands White Bone Pagoda, so named because of the piles of human bones fished from the river at this terrible spot.

In the days of sail the journey through the gorges, which took five days downriver, could take as many as fifty days against the currents. Teams of trackers, as many as four hundred strong, hauled the boats upstream. They scrambled along precipitous paths, wet in summer and icy in winter, pulling on hawsers of plaited bamboo as thick as a man's arm and a quarter of a mile long. A drummer on the boat kept them moving in time, and foremen skipped back and forth encouraging them with whips. It was not uncommon for entire teams, struggling for footholds and harnessed to a laden boat bucking in some of the fiercest currents known to navigators, to be plucked from the cliffs to sudden death.

The sailor had not appeared since morning, when we entered the gorges, and after supper I went to look for him in the fourth class cabins, picking my way through the steerage passengers lying in the corridors and the stairwells. I found him in his bunk in the stern, despairing. He looked ashen and damp. He was a seasick sailor, he confessed in a whisper. He was worried about the professional consequences.

"What will it mean?" he cried.

I struggled to underplay the implications of seasickness for a naval career.

"Perhaps you could get a desk job," I ventured at last.

He misunderstood desk for deck and sobbed into his pillow. "You cannot understand," he wailed.

He brightened considerably when the starlets arrived on a wave of perfume, on their way to the dance in the second class dining-hall. They teased him about feigning illness to avoid the dance. As if to prove them right, he sat up, distributed fruit and regaled us with stories of Shanghai, the picture of rude health. When they departed with a swish of nylon he seemed to deflate.

"You must go," he said emphatically. "Dance with the film girls. I think they like you."

The second class restaurant had been transformed into a dance-hall with two flashing lights and a cassette of waltz tunes. The dance was an echo of the Bund in Shanghai, the same tunes of another age, the same grave faces, the same careful, slightly jerky steps. It was a scene I was to find all the way across China. There was always something heart-rending about it, this ballroom dancing so far from ballrooms.

The starlets danced with each other, while I watched from the back of the room. The sailor would be disappointed.

Later we moored for the night off Badong. The grey roofs dripped into the streets while clouds unfurled through the orange groves. The town grew dark beneath sinking skies and a skeleton of lights emerged in the wet gloom. A dog barked somewhere.

Along the gangways of the boat the lights had been extinguished and the boat was quiet. Even the gamblers had retired. The only light was from the starlets' cabin. I had noticed they left it burning all night, as if they were afraid of the dark. Passing their open door, I could see them stretched out on their bunks, dozing over cheap paperbacks, their skirts pulled up around their thighs.

I stood at the rail listening to the river lapping the boat. One of the starlets emerged from her cabin and, seeing me, came up the gangway. I was surprised when she spoke to me in English in a flat American accent. She was fluent but ungrammatical, as if she had acquired the language herself, untutored.

Hesitantly she asked about visas, a common concern in China. Could she get a visa for America? When I answered politely if unhelpfully, a flood of questions and anxieties followed. They concerned a man in Florida, and his imminent visit. She twisted her hands around the rail. "I don't know it," she kept repeating. "I don't know it." Distress disguised itself beneath a nervous giggle.

She had met him three years ago when he was working on a six-month consultancy for a new sewage system in Chengdu. It was unclear what the nature of their relationship had been. He wrote frequently; she had a bundle of bedraggled airmail envelopes. Now he was coming to see her. She spoke as if he were coming to marry her, and she was desperate for my advice. I was no longer the pointless stranger. I was now the interpreter for another race, or at any rate for a sewage engineer in his mid fifties.

Through the gauze of the girl's anxieties and contradictions, the American proved a shadowy figure. She thought he was divorced or widowed. He was 25 years older than she was, and lived in Orlando. The suburban home, of which he must have sent photographs, was more sharply defined than its occupant, who hovered somewhere between the fitted kitchen and the den, an unknown quantity.

The gloom of the gangway, the sleeping boat, seemed to release her from caution, and she spilled out the story like a confession. He sent her money. The trip to Shanghai, the second class cabin, the clothes, the make-up were all funded from Orlando. But now the man himself was coming, and the comfortable security that the money had supported was thrown into turmoil.

She was full of questions of protocol on which I had to arbitrate. Should he stay in the flat she shared with her mother, or another flat she might borrow from a friend? The friend's flat was not very central but it had constant hot water. On the other hand, her mother's flat was more comfortable, and there was a television. She pleaded for advice, and I tried to steer her away from "television with mother," towards "hot water without mother." She was terrified of gossip and evaluated the neighbours on a complex scale of nosiness.

On one issue she was adamant. He must go immediately to the hospital for a test for AIDS. She had read a great deal about the problem of AIDS in the West. "Do you have this AIDS yet?" she asked, demurely.

Now and then she paused in the breathless rush of questions and gazed down at the dark water. Her face suddenly looked older, and much wiser than the questions implied. Love was not a part of her enquiry. It was not arriving from Orlando. Her questions were practical, as if happiness lay in a delicate balance of prosaic considerations.

"Do you want to marry him?" I asked.

She shrugged as if the question was irrelevant. "I don't know it."

"Do you think you will?"

She wrinkled her nose. "I don't know it. Foreigners are strange." She seemed to have forgotten for the moment that I was one.

"You mean strange looking?"

She nodded. "And they smell," she said.

It was a commonplace that, to the Chinese, westerners smelt unpleasant. "What do we smell of?" I asked.

She began to giggle. "Pigs," she blurted out. "They smell of pigs." She bent forward giggling uncontrollably, her hand clamped across her mouth, stifling the sound in a series of agonized gasps, the gesture an echo of the girl on the quai in Shanghai.

Beyond the gorges the city of Chongqing rears above the river like another petrified legend, bizarre, misshapen and glowering. It straddles a steep ridge between the Yangtze and its tributary, the Jialing. In this unnatural confinement the city is like a game of snakes and ladders with stairways leading to upper districts and steep streets slithering down again. Funicular cars rattle between vertical neighbourhoods, alleyways end in sudden precipices and glimpses of streets two hundred feet below, and the back doors of houses open into space. It is the only city in China without bicycles; no one could cope with the hills. A grimy smog squats over the city, tasting of soot. When the sun comes out in Chongqing, they say, the dogs bark.

It was not a place to linger. I arrived in the morning and bought a ticket, with surprising ease, for the afternoon train to Xi'an. With its sense of lives stacked on top of one another, all moored to this gloomy city, Chongqing depressed me. In the station among the crowds and the baggage and the farewells my heart lightened. On the train, pulling away into an unknown countryside, I felt at home.

Three

DREAMING OF HORSES

I shared my compartment with a professor of metallurgy. He was a charming man, shy, civilized and erudite, with the innocence of the academic. Iron ore may have been a passion but so were cinema and Tang ceramics. He could draw me a plan of our locomotive to illustrate steam generation, but he had difficulty mastering the window catches in our compartment.

Metallurgy, the professor confessed, had been kind to him. It had taken him as far as Winnipeg, a place for which he had an unaccountable enthusiasm. He reminisced about the grain elevators, the picnic coolers and the cars as big as living rooms. He spoke most fondly of hot dogs. He was delighted to find I too had been to Winnipeg, and seemed to feel that the Canadian prairies formed some bond between us.

Tilting through the red hills of Sichuan, we went to dinner. The *maître d'* sat at the door of the dining car like a bouncer, slovenly to the point of caricature: a sweaty man in an unbuttoned shirt, a cigarette glued to his lower lip. When we bought our meal tickets he lowered his legs to let us pass, bawling our order to the galley at the far end of the carriage. Mine included my identification: "bean curd, fish and rice for a foreign devil," as if it required special demonic ingredients. The two cooks, stripped to the waist, juggled meals in an inferno of flames and sizzling woks while vegetables and lumps of coal lay about their feet in a sooty confusion.

The train's long rope of smoke flapped at the window, part of the landscape. Beyond, old women were driving their buffaloes home along red lanes. Poplar trees, knee-deep in crops, fluttered like prayer banners above ancient villages strewn with geese and children. Around a long cambered curve we entered a bowl of hills where the late sun had polished the rice paddies a dull bronze. The shadows were lengthening in a world of bicycles and bullock carts and upturned roofs.

Over fish bones we talked about the films of Zhang Yimou, about Canadian rodeos, and finally about the Heavenly Horses.

Throughout the history of Eurasia, nomads have erupted from the heart of the continent with the unpredictability of tropical storms. Mobile, impulsive and warlike, people of no fixed abode, they were the bogeymen of Eurasia, feared by every civilization from ancient Greece to Mauryan India. They drank mare's blood for breakfast, wore animal skins and lived in the saddle. When they went to war they swept all before them. The nomadic threat from the steppes reached a spectacular climax in the fourteenth century with the Mongol hordes and Genghis Khan.

What made the nomads such a potent military force was their horsemanship. While settled peoples tended cattle and built villages, nomads tamed horses and crossed continents. The classical myths of the centaur began with the nomadic Scythians who sat their mounts so beautifully that, to the amazed Greeks, man and beast seemed to be one creature.

Four thousand miles to the east, the Chinese too envied the marvelous horses of the barbarians. In the second century BC when the envoy of the emperor Wu Di returned from the first mission to the western regions, where he had sought alliances against the Hsivng-nu, nomads who would later appear in European history as the Huns, nothing so intrigued the Chinese as his tales of horses. He told of the horses of Ferghana, a tall splendid breed, said to be descended from heavenly stock, akin to the dragon horses of Chinese legend. The mythologies of Asia are full of legendary horses, sacred steeds who could carry their riders to immortality. The Chinese now believed they had discovered them.

The first journeys along the road that Freya Stark has called "the oldest, the longest, the most romantic and the most persistent of all the chequered streams of trade," the road we have come to know as the Silk Road and the Chinese knew as the Journey to the West, were prompted by the desire for these horses. Embassies were sent westward, year after year, to bargain for them. When they proved fruitless, a military expedition was launched. A force of 60,000 men, with a further 100,000 in logistical support, crossed half of Asia in order to obtain breeding pairs of these heavenly horses. Some historians pour scorn on the idea that these missions had quasi-religious aims. They rightly point out that the Chinese desire for a larger breed of horse had a military purpose, that their quest was not so much for immortality as for victory over the well-mounted nomads who harried their borders. But the two ideas are not mutually exclusive, and the texts of the period insist on the spiritual dimension.

With the acquisition of these thoroughbreds, the Chinese seemed to feel they had completed some pact with the gods. A hymn captured the fevered anticipation that now swept China:

The Heavenly Horses are coming,
Riding from the Far West,
Across the drifting deserts
Now the barbarians are conquered . . .

The Heavenly Horses are coming . . .
They will carry me aloft
To the holy mountains of K'un-lun.
The Heavenly Horses have come
And the dragon will follow in their wake.
I shall reach the Gates of Heaven.
I shall see the Palace of God.

In this yearning, the Silk Road was born. Trade, politics, imperial adventurism, religious pilgrimages, all came later. In the beginning there was the dream of fine horses, of salvation. For the next 1,500 years they pranced through Chinese art, larger than life, bounding across frontiers.

Somewhere in the night we were joined in our compartment by two more people. From my lower bunk, in the dim light from the station, I could see only their legs: a pair of nondescript grey trousers and a pair of nylons and high heels. Later, as the train pulled out of the station, I opened my eyes and found myself looking at the woman now lying on the bunk opposite. She gazed back at me, the shadows quickening across a face that was young, beautiful and shrewd.

In the morning I found them both asleep. The woman lay curled beneath a pink bath towel. The man, a paunchy fellow with a pock-marked face and a grubby shirt, slept sitting upright, his head tilted back against the wall, his mouth ajar. The posture made him look as if he was paying obeisance to two shiny suitcases on the luggage rack above him. In a land of shabby luggage, such cases were a sign of considerable status, at odds with the coarse appearance of their owner.

At Guangyuan the man was awoken by a jerk of the train. Opening his eyes, he lowered his gaze from the suitcases to me.

"American?" he asked, hopefully.

The woman stirred, shifting her legs beneath the pink towel. He glanced down but decided against disturbing her. Instead he hawked loudly, leaning forward to deposit the results of this excavation on the floor between his feet. Surprised to find a carpet, he sucked the mouthful of phlegm back from his lips and went out to find a more suitable depository in the corridor.

Refreshed, he returned to the compartment voluble and eager to impress. He worked for a meat production company, and gave me his card. It had embossed gold lettering. It was a job which offered many Opportunities, he said, in a voice which implied that I, as a man of the world, would understand. But before I could enquire about the Opportunities he veered off into Sidelines. Sidelines were the thing, he confided. He had a number of them: videos, furs, and nipples.

"Nipples?" I asked hesitantly.

"Nipples, nipples," he said, twiddling his thumb and index finger rather roughly in mid air. "People are crying out for grease nipples."

The nipple-man was typical of many of China's new entrepreneurs. Economic reforms had opened the door to private enterprise, and China was full of folk tales of watermelon salesmen and taxi-drivers who had become millionaires in this new phenomenon, the free market. The great mass of people, accustomed to the iron rice bowl—a job for life—and wary of exposing themselves in what might prove to be only a temporary shift in Party philosophy, were slow to pursue openings in the market place. Such risks tended to attract the reckless, even the criminal—those with little to lose. It was a new frontier, and inevitably the frontiersmen were cowboys, not settlers.

Throughout his litany of Sidelines and Opportunities, the nipple entrepreneur was distracted only by the woman beside him sleepily rearranging herself beneath the pink towel. When a stockinged leg or bare arm escaped he covered them again carefully, as if they were goods that might spoil in the sunlight.

Eventually she work with a start, and sat up. She was dishevelled and confused. She looked at us and the compartment as if trying to remember where she was. Then she fumbled for her shoes beneath the seat, took up a sponge bag, and disappeared up the corridor without speaking.

"Have you been married long?" I asked

He looked at me as if weighing something up.

"A week," he said. "We are coming from my woman's village." That was the term he used: *wodenuren,* my woman—not the more usual airen, my wife or loved one.

Beyond the window peasants were trudging along dusty lanes with hoes over their shoulders. Villages rose above the endless cornfields like islands stranded at high tide, crumbling at the edges.

"Drudgery," the man said, gazing at the fields. "They will do anything to escape. They lack Opportunities."

"Is your wife from a farming village?" I asked.

"Who?"

"Your wife."

"Yes, yes. Her people are very poor. I paid her father a big bride price, and he was very happy." He looked at me through narrowed eyes. "She is not my wife, actually," he went on. "She is my concubine. I paid the bride price to the father, to keep him happy. But I have not married her."

He was pleased with his confession. He seemed to feel it had elevated him in my eyes. We were men of the world; women were another Opportunity.

"I thought concubines were illegal," I said. "They went out with the last emperor."

He shrugged. 'No one cares. Her father is happy with his money. The girl won't make trouble. She will be sweet, hoping I will marry her."

The professor returned from his self-imposed exile in the corridor. He was a paragon of oriental manners, concealing his distaste for the entrepreneur. To the chagrin of China's reformers, the professional classes, the benefits of economic liberalization seem to have been reaped by men who are little better than legalized black marketers, while the professions continue to subsist on depressed state salaries.

At Baoji the train sighed into the station between platforms of dense crowds. Passengers got down to stretch their legs and buy provisions: jars of fruit, greasy roast chickens, packets of instant noodles, cakes and ale. The entrepreneur lumbered away down the corridor in search of his wayward concubine.

Suddenly there was a hammering on our window. The professor and I looked round to see the girl gesturing frantically from the platform. The professor, hitherto a retiring fellow, suddenly revealed himself as the decisive man of action. He leapt to his feet and grabbed the girl's bag from the rack. Unable to master the window catch, he rushed out into the corridor and ran towards the carriage door. I looked out in time to see him throwing the bag down to the girl as the train jerked and pulled away. A moment later she had disappeared into the crowds.

The professor returned calmly and took his seat. "I believe she must have changed her mind about her destination," he said.

Presently the entrepreneur arrived, flustered and breathless. He looked around the compartment, at the pink towel crumpled in a corner, at the professor and myself, until his gaze finally alighted on the empty space in the luggage rack.

"Have you seen my wife?" he asked in a shrill voice.

The professor looked at him for a moment. "She was here a moment ago," he said absently. "I don't know where she's gone. Perhaps she is in the toilet." I felt a growing respect for metallurgists.

The entrepreneur rushed into the corridor again. He did not reappear until Xi'an where, from the platform, I saw him in the compartment collecting his shiny suitcases. The girl and her father had conducted a sophisticated sting. When the nipple entrepreneur turned up in their village of drudgery, they had recognized Opportunity knocking. I hoped the bride price had been high.

In the West the Silk Road led to many cities—Aleppo, Petra, Ctesiphon, Constantinople, Rome. In China it was more selective. Once through the high passes of the Pamirs and Karakorams the network of roads converged on two routes, one north and the other south of the deserts of Turkestan. As they approached the Great Wall and the boundaries of China the two became one in a long straight descent down the Gansu corridor to a single destination: the city of Xi'an. When the merchant caravans shuffled through its western gate, grey with the dust of the Gobi, they had arrived.

In its day Chang'an, as it was then known, was the largest and most cosmopolitan city in the world. Capital to more than eleven Chinese dynasties, it reached its zenith under the Tang between the seventh and the ninth centuries. Rome and Constantinople paled by comparison. Chang'an's population was nearly two million; its walls were 22 miles in circumference; its streets were full of merchants and craftsmen from across Asia—Turks, Persians, Koreans, Arabs, Japanese, Indians, Malays, Bactrians, Mongolians, Armenians—all drawn by the sophistication and opportunities of a city that was the talk of provincial towns from the Pacific to the Mediterranean.

The glories of its past are enshrined in the imperial tombs, which include the Terracotta Army, scattered through the yellow fields of the surrounding countryside. In the city, the ancient Ming walls, dark as gravestones, brood above a grid of leafy boulevards. History has shifted its attention elsewhere and Xi'an is now as provincial as Rome.

The city has aged beautifully. It has a languid quality. In the still afternoons the streets smelled of dust and blossoms. When the evenings unfurled through the old city gates, on waves of birdsong and charcoal smoke, cooking stalls sprouted on the pavements, serving kebabs and bowls of spicy noodles. Late into the night their red-shaded lamps dwindled down the long straight avenues like navigation lights to the dark suburbs.

But if I loved Xi'an, it was because of the people I met there.

At lunch one day I met a tutor from the Art Institute. Liu had the delicate whiskered expression of a hedgehog puzzled by daylight. He snuffled over his mutton stew, and invited me to view his students' work. The Institute was old and dilapidated, a series of dark rooms and narrow flagstoned courtyards. Bamboo screens hung in the tall doorways. The paintings, in traditional style, were paintings of paintings, derivative and formulaic. Liu introduced them according to their historical period: "this in the style of the Song dynasty, this in the style of the Tang dynasty." Many were beautiful. But their achievement was limited to the mastery of technique and style. Individual artistic vision had no place here.

"If there is something you like?" Liu hovered at my elbow. The academic had turned salesman. China's free market had made everyone a hustler.

I reminded him I was planning to cross the Gobi desert and didn't need a painting strapped to my bag. Like a conjuror, he proceeded to show me how huge sheets of rice paper could be folded to the size of a postage stamp. When it was clear I wasn't to going to venture into the art market he reverted with some relief to his role of genial host, and ordered tea.

Back in the main room, we found a young woman looking through a catalogue. In the gloom the light from the doorway lay along her forearms in liquid strokes. After the paintings with their subtle washes of colour, this sudden chiaroscuro was startling.

"Ah, here is our best student," Liu said.

Her name was Fu Wen. She came forward to greet me. She was quite tall for a Chinese. Her hand was cool and weightless.

"Is any of the work yours?" I asked her.

She led me to a painting on the far wall. It was a wide landscape, a river and mountains, full of rain. A group of figures, dwarfed on the river bank, were bowing to each other in farewell, while a boat was prepared for departure. In the middle distance, in a fold of wet hills, was an inviting house, its windows brimming with lamplight.

"It's beautiful," I said. "Has it a title?"

"'Farewell at Jingtai'," she said. She stood with her weight rolled forward onto the balls of her feet, as if on the verge of movement.

Someone had brought tea and a watermelon.

"Please, please," Liu said, motioning to chairs.

The light, through the bamboo screens, fell in narrow lines across her face. She was very beautiful. Her neck was long and slim as a colt's and her mouth pushed downwards when she smiled.

Liu cut the watermelon into sloppy pieces and we leaned forward, dripping juice and seeds onto the stone floor. Fu Wen threw back her head, brushing her hair out of her eyes with sticky fingers, laughing. It seemed the most marvellous sound in the world, this sudden infectious laughter. When I tried to decline another piece, she cried in English, "One more, one more," laughing, her face tilted up. For each piece I made a mock refusal, just to hear her laughing.

Liu had been called away to the telephone. Alone together, our appetite for melon suddenly disappeared. The rinds lay like capsized canoes about our feet.

"I did like the painting," I said. "Is it for sale?"

"No," she said, without explanation. After Liu's ardent commercialism, this lack of interest was a relief. She shook juice from her hands.

"Where will you go after Xi'an?" she asked. The laughter was gone and the question seemed almost aggressive.

"Through Gansu to Xinjiang. I am going to Kashgar."

"That is a sad journey," she said.

"Why?"

She shrugged. "For Chinese, I mean. It is a journey for foreigners. For Chinese, Xinjiang is not a place to visit."

"Where are the people going in your painting?" I asked.

She smiled. "They are going home."

We washed our hands under a tap in the courtyard and she saw me to the door. In the stone lobby she shook my hand, then said she hoped I would come and visit them again.

In the street, amongst the crowds in the dying afternoon, I felt suddenly and foolishly bereft.

Four

A NIGHT AT THE OPERA

The Silk Road was China's chief dalliance with the world beyond the Wall, an indiscretion that went on for centuries. The big-nosed foreigners brought little to their hosts in the way of practical advice. The Chinese had already invented most things: printing and paper, gunpowder and the mechanical clock, deep drilling and the paddle-wheel boat, seismographs and winnowing machines. But while China has always excelled at the practical, metaphysics was another matter. Contrary to some western perceptions, China is not a kingdom of philosophical speculation. Religion poured into China along the Silk Road like air into a vacuum.

For people faced with their own mortality, China's two contributions to metaphysical discussion, Confucianism and Taoism, offer little consolation. Confucianism, despite its temples and quasi-priesthoods, is not a religion but a social code. When it does address theology, it goes no further than the folk religion of ancestor worship. Taoism is a theology so nebulous that even the existence of God appears to be a hazy issue. In his absence, ritual has mushroomed and the modern religion seems to be held together with a miasma of gongs, incense and magic spells.

Buddhism and Islam both arrived in China with the pack animals and the footsore merchants of the Silk Road. Islam, with its appealing certainties, has left substantial communities of Muslims throughout western China. Buddhism, with its promise of reincarnation and nirvana, was an even bigger hit and spread through the whole country to become a substantial religious force. Having survived the onslaught of the Cultural Revolution, it is now enjoying a revival.

In the southern suburbs of Xi'an stands the Big Goose Pagoda, so called because its namesake in India marked the spot where a dead goose fell out of the sky. This must be a fairly routine event for dead geese, but the monks who witnessed its demise, possibly light-headed from chanting, decided the ex-goose was a saint and set about building. It is the kind of episode which can give religion a bad name.

Xi'an's pagoda and its adjoining temple were built in the seventh century to house the Buddhist scriptures brought back from India by Xuan Zang, the most renowned of Silk Road travellers. His journey across the Gobi desert and over the passes of the Pamirs, in contravention of the imperial edict forbidding foreign travel, was a remarkable odyssey during which he survived assassination attempts, hunger strikes, desert djinns and the lavish banquets of Central Asian princes. The story is one of the great Chinese romances, and the inspiration for the legend of the Journey to the West which Wang had pointed out on the temple roof in Shanghai.

I went along to the Big Goose to see the portrait of the man in whose footsteps I would be travelling. In the temple halls the Buddhas were plump childish figures with blue-rinsed hair and scarlet lips. Worshippers planted handfuls of incense in racks then shuffled inside to bow and leave offerings. The Buddhas, apparently, were partial to sweets and Marlboro cigarettes. In the pagoda elderly monks were wheezing up the long stairways, pausing to catch their breath on the landings before starting on the next flight, like beings attaining another level in the cycles of reincarnation.

Reaching the top they gazed down through sad cypress boughs at stupas packed with the bones of thirteen centuries of their fellow monks.

Xuan Zang's portrait was carved in grey stone, life-size, on a lower landing. Far from the swashbuckling hero one might expect, the great traveller looked like a chap who would have difficulty running to catch a bus. He had the flabby face and pot belly one might have expected of a court eunuch, and wore a rather fetching frock and an antique backpack—presumably another early invention of the Chinese. From an overhang above his head a small lantern was suspended to light his way.

Xuan's journey to India was a literary quest. Buddhism had already taken root in China, often in the face of official opposition, but religious study was handicapped by considerable confusions about texts. As it made its way along the Silk Road meanings and translations had often suffered from a kind of Chinese Whispers. In India Xuan loaded a caravan of twenty-two horses with Buddhist scriptures and brought them home for translation. You could not help but like the man. He crossed half of Asia, not for gold or for conquest, but for second-hand books.

In the Shaanxi museum the galleries were full of horses. The other exhibits—agate wine cups, jade seals, golden bowls, silver censors, stelae recording the history of China—all paled to nothing in the presence of these magnificent creatures. Smooth-flanked and long-legged, with necks like dancers and heads like gods, the horses stampeded through the galleries unchecked. Many were muscular and thickset with broad rumps and wide saddles, yet seemed weightless as dreams. Corralled into frescos and bas-reliefs, stabled in gold and bronze and glazed ceramics, they stamped and reared like creatures possessed. Galloping, they seemed to sprout wings.

A rainbow-coloured stallion, hooves outstretched, bore a young man across the crests of waves. Polo horses soared across a field, their riders leaning forward, each confident of a strike. An ochre-coloured mare pulled up, head turned, listening, alert and elusive. Three horses flew across a stone tablet, their manes streaming like banners, their hooves barely touching the ground, their flanks shining with sweat. One had an arrow through its heart, yet did not break stride, as if it had already passed into another realm.

These horses were not symbols of power so much as icons of worship, the cousins of the white stallions of pre-Roman England scribed on chalk hills. They were the descendants of the Heavenly Horses which Wu Di believed would carry him to Paradise. Their riders sought deliverance. Wishes danced beneath their hooves like sparks. They consumed roads and mountain passes and desert leagues in a tilting horizonless world. Their journeys were a flourish of arrivals. Departure existed only as escape: a clatter of hooves, a tossed mane and a sudden unencumbered freedom.

A plaque at the entrance identified the museum as an old Confucian temple. I tried in vain to imagine these rooms hushed and scented, gongs ringing in the courtyard, attendants padding in and out. The Confucian gods were Order and Duty. They must suffer an unquiet eternity in the presence of these horses, stampeding through their ancient halls, the very demons of the Confucian world. Willful and impulsive, they were the stuff of dreams. They were horses to bear you away.

I stayed until closing time when the attendants went through the courtyards ringing bells, like returning monks. The sound followed me out into the darkening streets. As I cycled up Nan Daije my trusty Flying Pigeon bicycle, hired for five pence an hour, felt positively equestrian. The handlebars became reins and the pedals stirrups. It was familiar territory: the bicycle horses of childhood. It felt like old times to be back in the saddle.

I galloped through an ancient archway, where cyclists veered away from each other in the gloom, and emerged into the street of the Art Institute. I had come this way with the idea that I might stop at the Institute on some pretext, but as I neared it I felt my courage failing me.

Remarkably, as I passed the building, Fu Wen was emerging with two friends. She had seen me, and came across to the kerb, smiling when I drew up. Suddenly any doubts vanished.

We shook hands with an awkward formality.

She asked where I was going.

"The opera," I blurted out, surprising myself.

Fu Wen clapped her hands with glee and said they would take me. Which opera was I going to?

"Any opera," I said. "With singing."

She turned and spoke to her friends but they were reluctant. It was late. They wanted to eat. For a moment Fu Wen hesitated. To go with me un-chaperoned would be to expose herself to gossip.

Then, wonderfully, she bid her friends good-night, and turned her bi-cycle to join me.

Outside the east gate of the city walls, in a narrow park between the ram-parts and a canal, opera was performed each evening in an atmosphere rem-iniscent of Elizabethan theatre. Lanterns hung in the trees and the audience, mainly old people, sat on low benches before a makeshift stage. The men waggled their fans and pulled their trousers above their knees to reveal hair-less legs. The old women smoked cigars stuck upright into clay pipes. Every-one sipped jars of tea in which the leaves floated like seaweed. It was a jolly social occasion for which the opera offered a stirring backdrop. Fu Wen and I joined the crowds standing around the periphery with their bicycles.

The performance was stylized, almost ritualistic. The characters, swathed in layers of tawdry silks, tottered across the plank stage on block sandals, nodding beneath tiered headgear. Long pheasant-tail plumes bobbed in their wake. Their faces were garish masks of make-up. Every detail conveyed meaning. Red cheeks indicated loyalty, white suggested cunning. A gesture conjured armies. Another carried the action from the battlefield to the palace. When the actors took to imaginary horses, their cavalry status was declared with pretty feathery whips. Long journeys were described by walking in circles.

The usual conspiracies of theatrical illusion seemed unimportant here. The orchestra—five old men in their vests—sat down stage, sawing away on two-stringed viols and clashing tinny cymbals like extras who had forgotten their costumes. Between acts the singers strolled through the crowds making assignations. Characters who had died in the preceding act turned up in the interval, in full costume, selling ice lollies. On stage their children, toddlers in crotchless pants, got under the feet of invading armies. Boredom was rife among the spear-carriers, who spent their time mouthing comments to friends in the audience. One fell asleep against a pillar and had to be woken to be slain in battle.

With our heads inclined together, Fu Wen told me the story as it unfolded. The cacophonous music, the garish faces, the trailing gowns, were reduced to something intimate between us. She rested her hand on my bicycle and told me of empires falling.

When it was over we drifted away through the park following the line of the walls toward the south gate. Along the empty paths, away from the crowds, Fu Wen grew animated. She sang scraps of opera. She laughed. She asked about my journey and when I told her about the Yangtze, she brimmed over with questions. Her eagerness was a kind of yearning. Yesterday, I marvelled, I had not even met this woman who now filled the evening. Through the dark trees I could see the lighted road on the other side of the canal where, with its bicycles and scooter trucks and roadside stalls, life appeared to be going on as before.

I rode her home, down a long avenue tunneling beneath plane trees into the southern suburbs. It was unlit except for the red lanterns of roadside stalls. Occasionally cars passed, their headlights illuminating the road, the trees, the dark shopfronts, like searchlights.

At a corner she stopped. Her house was nearby. She did not want me to see her to the door. We stood straddling our bicycles in the middle of the dark lane.

"Can I see you tomorrow?" I asked.

She thought for a moment. "In the afternoon," she said.

We tried to think where we could meet. Her need for discretion, her fear of gossip, limited the choices. She did not want to meet at the Institute.

"The Great Mosque," I said at last, "Two o'clock?"

She nodded. I leaned into the shadows and kissed her good-night, then she turned and cycled away. In the long avenue I was grateful for the navigation lights of the roadside stalls. I would hardly have known the way. Xi'an and China suddenly seemed so different.

In the morning the road to the Terracotta Army was fretted with sunlight. I had hardly slept, and set off early, happy for the distractions of an expedition to the beginnings of China, to the tomb of the man who built the Great Wall. A puncture delayed me briefly on the outskirts of town but a bicycle repair man, working from a cardboard box beneath a tree, fixed it for tuppence, throwing in a free service. I rode through a dusty landscape of haystacks and pomegranate orchards. Pink blossoms drifted in the lanes and the road was stained with fruit.

For centuries the large earth mound which marked the tomb of Qin Shiuhuang had attracted no more attention than the many other tumuli which littered the plains around Xi'an. Then in 1974 a farmer, digging a well in the corner of his orchard, struck something hard with his spade. When he cleared the loose earth he found not a rock but a clay head, the first glimpse of what was to be the most astonishing archaeological discovery of the century.

Excavation revealed thousands of life-sized terracotta soldiers, arrayed in battle formation, complete with horses and chariots, an honour guard for the dead emperor. After twenty years of digging there is still no end in sight. The 6,000 soldiers uncovered thus far may represent only a small fraction of the total army. Work has yet to begin on the tomb itself. The Chinese, typically, are taking the long view.

Ancient records describe the tomb of Qin Shiuhuang as a fabulous underground landscape. The ceilings were said to be inlaid with pearls to simulate the night sky. Trees were carved from precious stones. Gold and silver birds flitted among their leaves while rivers of mercury flowed beneath them. Historians were apt to dismiss these fantastical accounts, until the discovery of the Terracotta Army. Its scale suddenly makes anything possible.

The occupant of this extraordinary mausoleum ruled China for a mere fifteen years. The dynasty he founded did not survive his death. Yet his importance is undisputed. He was called the First Emperor. When he came to the throne in 221 BC he found a group of warring states. When he died in 207, he left behind a single nation, China, a corruption of the dynastic name Qin. He was a tyrant on the grand scale. He not only burnt books, he had their authors buried alive. He executed whole families for the crimes committed by one of their members. He conscripted thousands of workers for his endless building schemes and when they were disloyal enough to die on the job, he used their bodies as land-fill. Among his many projects was the construction of the Great Wall.

The army that was to protect him against the terrors of the underworld is now sheltered by an arena which protects it from the rain. Inside the soldiers stand in long trenches, rank upon orderly rank, a composed and confident company. Each statue is an individual portrait; of the 6,000, no two are alike.

They seem pleased at their resurrection, as if they had returned from a long and arduous campaign and were now basking, a little smugly, in the admiration of the crowds who turn out to greet them. Nothing lends them a sense of verismo so much as their duplicity, the familiar military conspiracy to hide the more grisly aspects of their victories. Like a real returning army, they present their best face to the world: the orderly ranks, the neat Edwardian beards, the untroubled brows, the faint smiles. These are, however, reconstructions. At the rear of the trenches, beneath canvas shrouds, lies a less picturesque reality. Here the figures are still encased in the earth. Heads, limbs, torsos, are jumbled together like broken china, the carnage of a bombed regiment, kept neatly out of sight of the admiring crowds.

I had lunch near the hot springs of Hua Qing, where generations of emperors built elegant pavilions and bathhouses. The Tang emperor Gao Zong spent so much time here dallying with his concubine, the fabled beauty Yang Guifei, that his ministers were obliged to have her assassinated in order to get him to concentrate on affairs of state. Hua Qing is full of such charming love stories.

After lunch I went for a bath in a local bathhouse that was like a cross between a boxer's gym and a cave. An attendant with a towel round his neck gave me a locker and I disrobed. Along a corridor I found naked Chinese men floundering through the steam. Whatever their age they seemed to have the bodies of adolescents, as smooth and slippery as seals. When I lowered myself into one of the two pools of creamy green water, its occupants fell silent then discreetly got out and climbed into the other. Later in the changing room, I looked round to find them gazing at me through a doorway, their faces twitching with curiosity.

I bullied my way onto a bus back to Xi'an, riding on the roof with my bicycle amid sacks of flour. In town I hurried to the Great Mosque, hidden in the winding lanes of the Muslim quarter. You turn a blind corner and fall into a garden of Chinese arches and pavilions, overblown flowers and old men with caged crickets. In its journey from the west Islam has travelled lightly, and the mosque has taken the form of a Chinese temple.

I could not find her at first, and was surprised at the strength of my dismay when I thought she had not come. But when I went back to the main gate there she was, waiting with her red bicycle, and all was suddenly well with the world again.

Fu Wen had not been to the Great Mosque before, and along the flagstone paths and through the grey-tiled pavilions she was suddenly the stranger and I the guide. I pointed out the Arabic inscriptions trailing like vines above a lintel. I explained about the cluster of shoes left outside the doors, the muezzin, the prayers which leaked into the daylight, and the traders who had come from Arabia and Persia more than a thousand years ago. I went on at such nervous length that she assumed I was a Muslim, and asked why I was not going to prayers.

In a small court off the main gardens, where potted ferns trailed over an empty fountain and birds gossiped in the rafters, we sat all afternoon talking, until the dark came. Among the frangipanis shedding their petals and the warnings of the muezzin, we were falling towards one another.

When the evening prayers were over the old men in their white caps drifted through the gardens to the communion of stone benches. Fu Wen buried her hand in mine.

"How long will you stay here?" she asked.

In my pocket I had a train ticket for the following day. I had already mentally discarded it.

"A week," I said. I had no idea.

"Where will you go then?"

"To Lanzhou. And then to Gansu."

At the base of her throat the small indentation, like a thumb-mark, trembled with her pulse. Her lips moved. Something unspoken waited inside her mouth.

"Come with me," I said. "Come to Tulufan. Come to Wulumuchi. Come to Kashi. I will meet you there. When can you come?"

She looked at me with narrowing eyes as if across a glare of distance. "It is not possible," she said.

I put my lips to the little spoon of skin, the soft pulse. She tilted her head back against a pillar, an equine arching. Her skin was buttery and smelt of almonds.

In the twilight the old men's pet crickets were singing their hearts out. They sang of love, the males and females serenading one another across the darkening gardens from their little wicker cages. Their duets could last for hours. In protracted litanies of offerings and responses, they were trying to identify and assess one another. If one of them departed from the melody by as little as a fourth of a tone, the exchange was abandoned, to be taken up again later with another. It was a quest for compatibility, the wisdom of crickets.

Her grandfather had been a landowner. It was not a large estate, a few orchards and small-holdings let to farmers on the edge of Xi'an, but it was to lie like a shadow across three generations of the family. In the land reforms after the revolution it was taken under state control as part of a communal farm. Her grandfather was fortunate. Many landowners, denounced by their tenants, were executed by revolutionary tribunals. He was simply stripped of his possessions. His tenants had been quite fond of him.

Her grandfather spent his remaining years ill and embittered. He complained that no one really cared for the land. They planted their crops and harvested them "like factory workers," he would say, with scant regard for the unproductive, the merely decorative. For him the land had a spiritual dimension. Ancestor worship is part of Chinese religious tradition, and the loss of the family estates was akin to the desecration of their graves. A few years after land reform the committee decided to chop down the orchards. They had been planted by his great-grandfather. The committee said the trees were past their best.

"Perhaps they were," Fu Wen said. "But he could never reconcile himself. He went in the evenings and sat on the stumps. My father had to go each night and fetch him home. He died of a broken heart."

In the new classless China, everyone was strictly categorized according to class background. It appeared on one's identity papers after name and date of birth. The children of peasants found themselves first in line for jobs, housing, education, while those with a bourgeois background were often denied preferment. The Party believed in a bloodline concept of guilt which held that the descendants of "bad elements" like landlords must carry the continuing stigma of their forbears' guilt. It was official policy until 1978.

When the mania of the Cultural Revolution began in the summer of 1966, her parents were students. In that fateful spring her father had the misfortune to come top of his class. Her mother's crime was potentially more serious. She wanted to be a writer, and had already had poetry and stories published in the local newspaper. These were to mark her out for special ridicule.

In the autumn term, study was abandoned in favour of rallies, public criticism and confessions. Teachers were denounced by their students and paraded through the streets in dunces' caps. In a particularly gruesome episode one of her father's tutors was paralysed for life when he was beaten up by the Red Guards for lack of zeal in his own self-criticism. Because he took no part in these persecutions Fu Wen's father immediately fell under suspicion. His good grades marked him out as an "élitist," addicted to competition. Meanwhile, at public rallies where the unrepentant were beaten, her mother was forced to denounce her own writing as bourgeois and counter-revolutionary.

In the midst of this madness they had married, hoping perhaps to recapture a private world beyond the grasp of public hysteria. It was a vain hope. In early 1968 they were sent to the countryside "to learn from the peasants." They were part of one of the greatest movements of population in history. Almost 17 million people were sent into internal exile, one in ten of the urban population. The peasants, regrettably, were not consulted and found themselves suddenly playing host to train-loads of weedy intellectuals who knew nothing about hardship and less about farming.

Though Fu Wen seemed a modern metropolitan woman, she had grown up in the country amongst mud and cabbages. She was born on a communal farm in a remote part of Gansu province, almost 700 miles to the west of Xi'an. At the time the family was living in half of a one-roomed house, a curtain dividing their living space from that of the village family who, until their arrival, had had the whole room to themselves. As the years passed, while they swilled out the pigs, ploughed the fields, and waited on the weather, her parents were trying to find a way back to Xi'an, to some shadow of their former lives. Long after the Cultural Revolution had subsided, its victims, in their millions, were still stranded in their places of exile all over China, unable to find their way through the labyrinth of permits, job searches, and housing queues that would take them home. Eighteen years after their departure, Fu Wen's family returned home to Xi'an.

With the help of her former tutors, Fu Wen's mother secured a post as a primary school teacher. Her father, who had been one of the brightest mathematical minds of his academic year, found a job as accountancy clerk in a shoe factory. They were assigned a flat in the southern suburbs. It stood on land that had once been part of her grandfather's orchards.

The years of zealotry had left the habit of protecting oneself against criticism, personal as much as political. Reputations were guarded like fortunes. Fu Wen was terrified of gossip.

I never went to the Institute again. Fu Wen telephoned me to arrange our assignations. We spent the afternoons in my hotel room, which we reached by the back stairs. When we hired a car to go out of town to visit the western tombs, she wanted to check first that the driver was not someone she knew. In the streets we found our steps turning to the empty avenues atop the city walls. The secrecy irritated me but for Fu Wen I think it became part of the excitement. In a life of constraints, the illicit flexes powerful muscles.

In the dwindling hours we had together, Fu Wen fussed over me, worried that I might become ill, that I would be lonely, that people would take advantage of me. She became maternal, arriving with packets of green tea and homemade dumplings. I was the hardened traveller, crossing half of Asia, and she grew tearful about my vulnerabilities. I admired her intelligence and her strength. She worried how I would cope.

In the afternoons in the hotel room with the curtains drawn we retreated into a world of our own creation, a landscape of limbs, a neutral territory with only two citizens, their divided loyalties happily disguised.

The hotel was opposite the railway station. The whistle of the trains, the shouts of the guards, the muffled announcement of destinations, crept into our world almost unnoticed. Later when we stepped outside into the crowds hurrying through the dusk we seemed to be infected with their collective anxiety about arrivals and departures. The people and the traffic, pressing homeward, broke the delightful sense of suspension in which we had passed the afternoon. Jogged into motion again, I felt us moving apart as if we were now on different trains.

In the crowded cafés of the Jiefang Market where we went for dinner, the sense of distance after the intimacies of the afternoon seemed unbearable. I rode her home along Chang'an Lu beneath the dark arches of the plane trees. Saying goodbye in the lane broke my heart every evening. When she cycled away into the darkness I longed to call after her, to call across the widening frontiers.

* * *

"It is a dream," she said. "Don't confuse this with real life."

We were on top of the city walls. We came here often to be alone. I was ripping up my notebooks to make paper aeroplanes which we launched from these empty heights into courtyards and back lanes, unobserved. Sheltering in the old pavilions, among the starlings and the litter of lovers, I realized we were hiding like truants, hiding from China. I flew a folded Concorde to her.

"I am twenty-eight," she said, jumping up to catch the paper glider. "All my school friends are married and have children. My parents are worried about me. They want to see me settled."

"What do you want?" I asked.

"I want to find a life where I can be happy." She sounded like a traveller turning homeward, that odd mix of resignation and anticipation. "We cannot be happy together. Only briefly, now." I felt like a child, standing there with my paper aeroplanes. I knew what she was saying, but I did not want to listen to it.

"Why should I give you my life?" she said. "You would not know what to do with it."

"I want to go home," I said.

We took a taxi to the hotel.

Five

TO THE BORDERS OF TIBET

As a stage for departures, Xi'an is in the same league as the Pillars of Hercules. For thousands of years Chinese have passed through its western gate with heavy hearts, embarking on journeys that would take them beyond the ordered and civilized world of the Celestial Kingdom, the Journey to the West. The stage has shifted form the western gate to the railway station but the drama is unchanged: family groups, last-minute additions to baggage, hurried advice, promises of return, tears, and flocks of hands fluttering farewell. My train was bound for Urumqi, the capital of Xinjiang, following the line of the old road towards the Gobi and exile. The characters were as predictable as the route: officials, soldiers and settlers embarking on a journey as old as China.

Fu Wen came to the station. The guards' whistles, the echoing announcements, and the hooting of the trains which had been the background of our afternoons together were suddenly loud and real. We stood in a corner of the vast concourse behind a magazine stall. She fussed over my bag, worrying I had forgotten something, checking I had not lost my ticket. Then suddenly she was withdrawn, her eyes welling with tears. She fell away from me, fingering a little scar on her hand. The disembodied voice was announcing my train.

"I am sorry to see you go, Stanley," she said. In five months in China no one else would say that to me. Then I was swept up in crowds hurrying towards the platforms.

In the carriage, amid the confusion of people looking for seats, I sat by a window watching the city slip away. Then I saw Fu Wen, standing with her red bicycle on the top of the city walls, a small figure with the still and dignified posture of the Chinese. She waved to the train. I tried to open the window so she would see me waving back but it was jammed. I watched her through the glass until the train curved and Xi'an disappeared.

West of Xi'an sorghum flooded the landscape, the ripe heads nodding in the heat. Here and there the crops parted to reveal white lanes where men in vests cycled beneath the shade of poplars. Goats and buffaloes slept together in the ditches. Walled villages floated above the fields, the same baked colour as the earth and the crops and the faces of the field-workers beneath their lampshade hats. We passed a river bed where villagers were bathing in silver streams, and the train surprised a man pulling on his trousers in the cover of tall reeds.

Set back from the railway were ridges crumbling into the sorghum which lapped their feet. In their loess faces were caves, many of them inhabited. Their mouths had been closed with low doors. The troglodyte communities went on for miles.

There are said to be thirty-five million cave-dwellers in China. A cave may not be the most fashionable of addresses, but there is much to commend it. Caves are cool in summer and warm in winter. Maintenance costs are low. Finally, in a country of such dense cultivation, they are the only form of housing which does not occupy arable land. Far from trying to re-house these troglodytes, the government has endeavoured to make a virtue of them, assigning committees of architects to study the situation. Their recommendation stands as a warning about committees: Larger Windows, they said.

In the dining car the spittoons slid back and forth bumping our feet. My dinner companions were a moon-faced couple in nylon shirts. They were on their way to Xinjiang to take up posts in a steel factory in Korla. They were settlers; their whole lives were in the baggage car. The man spat fish bones onto his plate, and talked excitedly about government incentives and housing benefits while his wife gazed out the window at the villages sailing in the sorghum, the exhausted sunflowers drooping by a wall, the poplars thin as smoke. Gazing out at China she began to sob over her steamed dumplings.

Later in the corridor the man apologized for his wife's tears. She was apprehensive, he said. "Xinjiang is like another country. We say it is 'outside the mouth'." The phrase conjured all the Chinese anxieties about the regions beyond the Great Wall.

With evening the train began to climb through loess hills. We followed the line of the river Wei, shining in the late sun as it turned between darkening slopes. The hills grew steeper and the train dove in and out of tunnels. The valley became a gorge and the river, far beneath us now, was the colour of wet clay. Villages clung to shelves of rock, their crops staggering down thin terraces. In a steep meadow two cows stood marble-white in the twilight, as still as statues.

We crossed into Gansu, a province as big as Texas. Dusk slipped down the hillsides and into the arms of the river. The evening was smoky. A half-moon sailed between pointed hills and the village houses spilled aprons of yellow light into the blue night.

I retreated to my bunk, thinking of Fu Wen. We had created our own country, and exile was bitter. I pictured her wonderful face, and her sudden smiles that always made my heart quicken. I cried, grateful for the darkened carriage. I felt like the woman over her dumplings, hurtling westward to unwanted frontiers, everything I cared for slipping away beyond the windows. On this dark train I felt terribly alone.

Hard sleeper, the middle of three classes on Chinese trains, is like a travelling army boot camp. In the long dormitory carriages, amid the tiered bunks festooned with laundry and kit bags, the passengers sit about like rowdy conscripts, playing cards and munching on rations while the detritus builds up about their feet: chicken bones, shells, water-melon rinds, empty beer bottles, tea-leaves, the whole morass glazed with phlegm. There is a camaraderie about hard sleeper. We looked out for one another and got up to things behind the backs of the sergeant-majors, the carriage attendants who descended occasionally with cruel brooms scattering all before them.

Reveille came early. At 4:30 a.m. the lights were switched on and the carriage speakers began to broadcast martial music at parade-ground volume. The Chinese, accustomed to the drill, stumbled groggily from their bunks while the sergeant-major collected their bedding. She did not look kindly on malingerers. Believing myself to be in the grip of an unsavoury military dream, I buried my head in my pillow. A moment later I felt someone clawing at my sheets. Before I could respond, sheets, blankets and pillow were snapped from me with a single powerful tug, leaving me stunned and trouserless on my bunk.

Next came slopping out. Ill-tempered from a short night, the attendants attacked the carriages with mop and bucket while the passengers retreated to the upper bunks. On my own bunk I was able to offer sanctuary to an old woman, a sack of incontinent geese, and three wailing children caught between the twin terrors of a foreign devil and the sergeant-major.

When the tides had subsided, I trekked to the end of the carriage for my morning ablutions. There my misery was complete. There was no water in the taps, the samovar had gone cold, the hot water flasks were empty, and the toilets had been locked by the sergeant-major. She did not want them sullied before the end of her shift at Lanzhou, still two hours away.

Only such hardships as these could make Lanzhou a welcome sight. In an ashen dawn I gazed out on a bleak industrial scene. Rows of chimneys belched over ramshackle suburbs. A coal-burning power station reared up just off the main street. Two giant slag heaps overlooked a public park. As we drew into the dark station we were confronted by a row of giant billboards. One advertised artificial limbs, a specialty of Lanzhou. Another advertised wheelchairs, presumably in the event of the limbs not being up to scratch.

The third was a message from the Party: Improve Sanitation For a Socialist Future. Keen to oblige I hurried towards the station but found that it too was mysteriously locked. Taking things in my own hands, I crossed the tracks and urinated on the billboard.

Strung out along the Yellow River between escarpments scarred by quarrying, Lanzhou is a narrow gloomy place. After Liberation the Communists decided to transform it into an industrial centre. The result is that it has become one of the most polluted cities in China. A yellow smog squats over the streets where the coughing inhabitants hurry past each other with depressed faces.

The hotel—a vast Soviet-style block—was a bright spot. I have a perverse affection for socialist art and architecture. Its aesthetic pedantry is ideally suited to the great tragedy of failed idealism. Lanzhou needed a bit of romance, and the hotel's proletarian grandeur supplied it. With its forecourt of black Shanghai sedans, its vast lobby beneath grimy chandeliers, and its hallways, broad and empty enough for political rallies, it had the cold dignity of a People's Palace.

In a garden which everyone but the gardeners seemed to have overlooked I breakfasted on the sweet buns which Fu Wen and I had bought the previous day for my journey. Then I wrote her a letter and tried to tell her how much I missed her. Already I felt her slipping away, her memory like water, running away between my fingers.

Lanzhou is the unlikely home of one of China's most famous figures, renowned both at home and abroad. In the great exhibitions which toured Europe and America in the early 1970s, he was the star turn. His image adorned publicity posters in London, Paris and New York. I can remember the long queues in the forecourt of the British Museum and the hushed anticipation as we made our way up the stairs and into his presence. International fame enhanced his position at home, and his image has been rather debased by becoming a symbol of tourism, like Michelangelo's David, appearing on everything from museum tickets to souvenir ashtrays.

He resides now in semi-retirement. In Lanzhou, visitors are few. So far as I know he no longer travels. The glory days of twenty years ago are a distant memory. He has become something of a recluse. Going to see him was like paying a call on a famous star of another era, a face familiar from endless re-runs, but now rarely seen in public.

I found him on the first floor of the Gansu provincial museum, a cobwebbed building of flint axes and agricultural exhibits. The galleries were empty and the attendants dozed in shafts of sunlight slanting between glass cases. I rounded a corner and suddenly there he was, slightly smaller than I remembered, but no less magnificent. Of all China's many images of the Heavenly Horses, he is the most remarkable. He ranks as one of the finest equestrian statues in the world, effortlessly the peer of the horses of San Marco, the Parthenon bas-reliefs, and Marcus Aurelius's mount on the Roman Capitol. He is a Chinese Pegasus, known popularly as *Fei Ma,* the Flying Horse.

He is patinated bronze, and stands just over a foot high. Like the Terracotta Army, he was a tomb figure. Behind him are arrayed the rest of the cortège—cavalry, chariots and attendants, almost eighty figures in all. The whole ensemble was discovered near Wuwei, in the tomb of a General Zhang which dates from the second century AD.

Lathered with verdigris, the horses have the deep chests of mounts who could gallop forever. They are restive, heads cocked, ears alert, their tails up. Their weight is thrown slightly back, as if they might rear at any moment. If they did so, it would be in unison, for the horses seem to share a collective consciousness, like dancers tuned to the same score. They are neighing, a great silent chorus.

The Flying Horse at their head is riderless, a common funeral tradition. Though its symbolism has become diffused, in second-century China this celestial horse had a clear purpose: it was to carry the dead man to immortality. Though *Fei Ma* is not winged, as the name might imply, he is weightless as a bird. Three of his hooves are in mid air; the fourth rests on the back of a swallow who looks round, astonished to find a horse amongst the clouds. *Fei Ma* too is neighing, his head thrown to one side. One imagines the sound as a kind of laughter.

Outside in the soupy twilight Lanzhou brought me back to earth. I was tired suddenly of urban China, its uniformity and its sourness. I wanted out of this shabby town. I longed for horses and landscape. I crossed the road to the bus station and booked a ticket to Xiahe. Tomorrow I would be in the grasslands, on the borders of Tibet.

In Lanzhou in the pre-dawn the Yellow River was as cloudy as the Milky Way whose tributary it is said to be. The bus was an ancient charabanc whose doors no longer worked, obliging the passengers to climb ignominiously through the windows. As it wheezed up the escarpment above the city it shook so violently, I feared for its disintegration. Once over the top we hurtled downwards into steep loess hills with an abandon born of poor brakes.

I now understood why the booking office had insisted I sign up for an insurance policy before they would sell me a ticket. The other passengers,

Buddhist pilgrims on their way to Xiahe's Labrang monastery, had opted for the comprehensive cover of religious faith. They gazed out the window with the equanimity of people who were on good terms with their underwriter.

I sat between representatives of the body and the soul, a doctor and a monk. The doctor was an anorexic figure with the kind of exuberant nasal hair from which it is impossible to tear one's gaze. When news of his profession got out, passengers queued in the aisle for treatment. They described the most frightful symptoms. The doctor, the very model of professionalism, folded powders—dried snake milk, rhino horn, frog scrotum—into little squares of paper and sent them away happy. When his travelling pharmacy was depleted, he resorted to mysticism. Borrowing my biro, he wrote cures on the squares of paper. His patients read the cure, then ate the paper. They brightened almost immediately.

The monk, wrapped in claret-coloured robes, was on his way home to the monastery form the bright lights of Lanzhou. He was a jolly fellow who shared his bag of nuts with me. He asked after "Ghantiperry," by which I assumed he meant the archbishop, in tones that implied I must know him personally. I said I hadn't seen him for a while.

Throughout the long afternoon the doctor and the monk slept contentedly on my shoulders. We crossed a rolling plateau where bashful sunflowers hid in fields of ripe corn and the wheat was stacked like witches' hats. The threshers were on to a good thing: they had spread the wheat on the road, then fallen asleep beneath birch trees while the traffic did their work for them. We passed brick kilns trailing ribbons of black smoke and carpenters working outside their shops, knee-deep in blond shavings. Sunlight poured through lanes of mimosa trees onto the blue tarmac and pink hollyhocks drooped over walls. The inhabitants of the villages along the road were a diverse lot—Turkic, Mongol, Chinese Muslims, Tibetans—many of whom had taken refuge in this remote corner of southern Gansu in the wake of the great upheavals wrought by Genghis Khan 700 years before. One village clustered around a mosque, the next was adorned with Buddhist prayer flags.

We passed an accident, a fearful tangle of vehicles with a gathering crowd. The driver of a truck still sat at his wheel, dead. A donkey lay in the road, looking puzzled, its neck broken. Near the base of one of the birch trees a coat covered a child-sized form. The pilgrims, contemplating nirvana, were unfazed. Our driver swerved to avoid a tractor and put his foot down, as if hoping to outrun misfortune.

At a crossroads we entered a long narrow valley. The road wound between a charcoal river and low cliffs in the middle distance. The fields had fallen away, and the landscape looked empty. The few houses were now all Tibetan with their high walls and distinctive carved doorways.

Xiahe lay stretched out on the banks of the river in the evening light. Wooden buildings lined its single street, the upper floors enjoying rather grand balconies. The ground floors housed crowded shops selling daggers, swords, saddles, rope, and yak-hair shoeliners. Robed monks drifted up and down the street like large burgundy bats. At the western end of the town stood the monastery, enclosed behind madder- and ochre-coloured walls, the magnificent gilded roofs of its temples melting in the last rays of the sun.

This corner of southern Gansu is known as Little Tibet because of its substantial Tibetan population. Most are Goloks, Tibetan nomads, who have migrated from the Tibetan plateau, only a few days' ride away, drawn to Xiahe by the good pastures and the monastery, one of six great institutions of the Yellow Hat Sect of Tibetan Buddhism. Their white tents dotted the surrounding hillsides.

The nomads rode into town on nervous ponies and shaggy yaks, hitching them to the telegraph poles along the main street. They were grubby glamorous figures in big hats. The women favoured stiff-brimmed sombreros. Their hair, shiny with yak grease and embroidered with coloured ribbons, hung to the waist over pink shirts and velvet capes. The men tended to old fedoras, fur-lined cloaks, felt boots and long daggers. Their faces were the colour of mahogany.

The Tibetans hated the shopkeepers, Chinese Muslims on whom both they and the monks depended for most of their material needs. Dowdy suspicious creatures, the Chinese hovered in the gloom of their shops, proprietorial amongst their wares. In the evenings their wives strolled together in the street in their Mao suits, knitting against the coming winter. The antipathy was mutual. To the shopkeepers the Tibetans were barbarians. The usual Chinese xenophobia was exacerbated here by Muslim abhorrence of Buddhist "paganism."

I stayed in the monastery guesthouse. It lay on the river bank beyond the town and had once been the summer residence of the Living Buddhas. Banks of sweet peas filled the courtyards and you could rent dilapidated bicycles from a Uriah Heep figure in a shed by the gate. Service was so slow in the refectory that I resorted to the eating-houses in town where they served up bowls of stew that made the lips of my fellow diners, Tibetan cowpokes, shine in the gaslight like oil slicks.

Throughout the town and out along the country tracks were small temples, as common as corner shops, where the nomads got down from their yaks to pray. The shrines looked like open-sided cattle sheds with fancy eaves. From their roofs tattered prayer flags fluttered, the banners of the kingdoms of the soul. In the long porticoes the pilgrims spun fat prayer drums as they passed on their endless perambulations. Adorned with sacred texts, the drums twirled prayers into the world, to compete with the birdsong and the wood smoke. The sound of the prayer drums squeaking on their metal axles pervaded Xiahe, a thin dogged complaint.

At its height Labrang monastery had housed nearly 4,000 monks or lamas. Like so many religious institutions in China, it suffered during the Cultural Revolution. The monks were forced to return to their home villages to work. The temples deteriorated, and in some cases were vandalized by the Red Guards. From this nadir the monastery is now reviving. Its population of monks is back to almost 1,500 and many of the great halls are under reconstruction. There is a vibrancy about the place, and a confidence born of hardship.

The Yellow Hats are a reforming sect whose monks, struggling to improve the reputation of monasteries, abandoned wine and women in the fourteenth century. Despite these privations the lamas of Xiahe seemed a jolly lot. As well as the monastery's more esoteric colleges—Theology, Debating, Tibetan Medicine—there is a School of Lama Dancing. Music is a popular pastime, and the lamas are sometimes to be seen on the banks of the river in the late afternoon sun, blowing their long ceremonial horns in informal jam sessions.

A young lama showed me through the temples, huge buildings with fortress walls and golden roofs. Inside, the gloom was lit only by wicks burning fitfully in bowls of yak butter brought by pilgrims. Electricity, a new idea here, is mistrusted since the Great Chanting Hall was gutted in 1985 in a fire caused by faulty wiring.

The decoration was overwhelming. Images of the Buddha were everywhere, from vast golden statues to intricate miniatures. Crowded around them were carved bodhisattvas, relics in wooden niches, huge wall tapestries, prayer flags, wood carvings, shelves of scrolls, more statues of Buddha—on and on it went, layer upon layer of artefact and imagery. For the pilgrim the very crowdedness of the temples was part of their reassurance. There were no empty spaces, no blank walls, no room for doubt.

On fine days I walked for hours through the grasslands to the west in a landscape of high meadows and wildflowers and nomad encampments. In the early mornings, ponds of shadow lay in the folds of the hills. The air was full of songbirds and yellow butterflies and the smell of dung fires.

One day a girl of eight with a huge pink bow in her hair came tumbling down a steep path to ask me to lunch in the tents above. She led me past the camp dogs, big as wolves, which she kept from devouring me with well-aimed rocks.

The girl's father was a magnificent fellow seated in a white tent full of brightly-painted trunks and beautiful daughters. He gave me a lunch of tsamba—a grey porridge that tastes of sawdust—and yak butter, a revolting substance that, as an honoured guest, I was obliged to eat in some quantity. Over ash-flavoured tea he complained about the lack of good husbands for his daughters. Apparently almost a quarter of Tibetan males enter the celibate priesthood. His daughters were all tall and slim with silver necklaces at their throats. Religion seemed a poor alternative.

Another day I met a Tibetan horseman bathing his feet in a stream, his pony grazing at his back. When I asked him where he was going he said Lhasa, as one might say the corner shop. It was almost 800 miles away. He had a face like leather and small shrewd eyes. He was a traveller and he quizzed me for some time about how I had come to this place. The trains fascinated him—he had never been on one—but we struggled a bit with the Yangtze boats. He couldn't see why they didn't sink. I flannelled a bit about displacement but finally agreed that I too was mystified by why all that iron floated. Mulling over these problems, he rode off toward the south and Tibet.

Later I came to a bowl of hills where three Chinese workmen were building a road. They lived in white tents pitched on the slope above the site. One was cooking rice while the others shovelled gravel. They said they did not know where the road was going. A surveyor came out from Lanzhou every week and marked out the next week's work. In this way week by week their road inched through these hills of nomads and horsemen towards the outer reaches of Tibet. The Chinese have come to realize that a road is a far more effective method of controlling nomads than a Wall.

* * *

One day in the Debating Square outside the temple of Maitreya I met the doctor. "Oh, oh," he hopped excitedly on one leg. "The Living Buddha, the Living Buddha. Tonight he is coming to your hotel."

The Living Buddha came to the hotel in a Toyota Landcruiser. He was a small boy of eight or nine years of age. He got down from the car into a scrum of elderly and august lamas, and the whole berobed crowd floated up the steps and into a large assembly room where they were met by Chinese officials, the local Party hierarchy. An evening of Tibetan entertainments followed. It was difficult to know who were the hosts and who the guests but whatever the arrangement it was a delicate *pas de deux*, this dance between Chinese secular power and Tibetan religious authority, full of smiles and courtesies and dark thoughts.

The monks had been allowed to return to Labang in 1980. For the Chinese, the monastery has its uses. It offers large-scale employment to young Tibetan males who might otherwise prove to be malcontents. Then too it is the chief engine of the local economy, and is seen as a potential attraction for tourists and thus a generator of foreign currency.

For the Tibetans, these have become levers with which they can press the authorities for larger grants, for a larger quota of lamas, for greater freedom. As in Tibet itself, the Chinese walk a tightrope, trying to encourage the monastery for their own reasons, while dampening the fever of Tibetan nationalism for which it is inevitably a symbol. The monastery now receives state grants for restoration but the authorities keep a strict cap on the number of monks.

The evening of entertainments broke up in some confusion when the power failed, as it did most nights, and the hall was plunged into darkness. The Living Buddha, the elderly lamas, the Party officials and the young Tibetan dancers all groped their way outside to the waiting cars. The sudden darkness had saved them the awkward ritual of saying goodnight.

* * *

It was a short train journey to Wuwei, only eight hours, so I decided to circumvent the usual difficulties of acquiring a ticket by travelling hard-seat, the lowest class on Chinese trains, lower even than army boot camp. It was a mistake.

In the station in Lanzhou I found my fellow hard-seat passengers, a dangerous looking mob, corralled by steel barriers and patrolled by formidable women with loudhailers. Machine-gun emplacements might have been more effective. With the announcement of the arriving train, the crowd bolted from their confinement, leaping the barriers and the women like Grand National winners. They hit the platform at full gallop.

Heavily armed with baggage the passengers fought their way aboard the train in a series of hand-to-hand skirmishes. People who had hoped to disembark at Lanzhou were carried deeper into the train where they were eventually obliged to break out through the windows. On this rising tide I was carried aboard like flotsam, coming to rest in the connecting passage between two carriages.

Here I spent the next eight hours enjoying the sort of intimacy with my fellow passengers normally reserved for the rugby scrum, the orgy, or the January sales. An old man lay crammed between my legs. Two soldiers were jack-knifed beneath my arms, a mysterious fellow with an oil drum and poor standards of personal hygiene was perched above my shoulder while a young mother, breast-feeding on demand, was pinned to my chest. Conversation was rather strained.

At Wuwei, the conductor beat a path to the door with a lathi and I got down onto an empty platform. Train passengers did not get out at Wuwei. They knew better.

Every afternoon a dust storm sweeps through Wuwei carrying the lacerating sands of the Gobi on a north wind, a ritual I liked to watch from the ramparts of the Bell Tower set above the ancient Dayan Buddhist temple. The birds announced its arrival by rising from their afternoon perches and swirling above the roof-tops like litter. Wuwei is a private town, enclosed behind high walls. As the winds began to batter the outside doors I could see the inhabitants scurrying about their courtyards snatching laundry from the lines, chasing chickens into coops and closing shutters. Only the old men in the temple gardens were unmoved, doggedly sticking to their mah-jong, as the dark clouds engulfed the town and the wind upset the empty chairs.

My hotel could have doubled as a penitentiary with its cement floors, its hard cots, its communal washing facilities, its grilled windows and its attendants patrolling with huge bunches of keys on their belts. Disembodied voices trundled up and down the bare corridors. Downstairs the carpeted lobby was occupied by a rather sinister collection of army officers, draped over armchairs and leaning in doorways. Their caps were brocaded like theatre curtains and they wore their coats on their shoulders like capes. They had a certain smugness, as if they knew the next radio broadcast would bring news of a military coup.

Wuwei was a pivotal point on the Silk Road, the commercial and political centre of the Hexi corridor which joined China to Central Asia. During the Tang dynasty passing caravans made it rich while the surrounding pasturelands were famous for their stud farms. It was a lively place where even the temples joined in the fun, boasting magicians, fire-eaters and acrobats. Xuan Zang enthused about its fine wines. Six centuries later Marco Polo, ever pedestrian, couldn't find much to remark upon beyond "an abundance of corn." One of its more famous residents was Kumarajiva who became, in Chinese Buddhist annals, the Nineteenth Patriarch. In the fourth century he spent seventeen years in Wuwei translating more than 300 volumes of Mahayana scriptures. His work is commemorated by the Kumarajiva Pagoda, a monument to words.

It proved a difficult building to reach. I could see it, rising above tangled roof-tops, but forays tended to end in blind alleys. It lay at the heart of the labyrinthine legal quarter, a leafy clutter of buildings that included the police headquarters, the court-house and the county gaol. On the paths between dusty marigolds and camphor trees policemen and prisoners strolled like lovers, handcuffed together, chatting and laughing amicably as they escorted each other from one building to another.

I was eventually led to the pagoda by a High Court judge. He was a cheerful fellow with his shirt knotted above his bare tummy and his trousers rolled up to his knees. He was on his way to try a difficult case which he described in English as "very grave, very murderous." Strapped to the back of his bicycle was the head of a freshly butchered cow. As he led me through the maze of alleys it left a trail of blood in our wake which I later used to find my way back to the main street. Its tongue lolled hideously between wet lips. The eyes followed me like the eyes of a portrait.

"You are from England?" the judge asked.

"Yes," I said, dropping slightly astern in the hope of shaking off the sorry gaze of the cow.

"The Old Boiling," the judge said. "Very famous. Number One court. Tell me. Do the judges in the Old Boiling Number One court still wear the women's hair?"

"Wigs. Yes, I am afraid so," I said.

The judge roared with laughter. "And women's dresses?"

"Absolutely. The judges are very fond of women's clothing."

He could hardly contain himself. In his hilarity he slapped the cow's forehead and the stiffening jaws closed slowly on the tongue.

The judge grew suddenly serious. "What about execution? Do you execute?" He made a chopping motion with his hand. It was, given the cow, a tasteless gesture.

"No," I said. "We gave it up. It didn't work."

"Didn't work?" he snorted. "What could be simpler? What method are you using? Shooting, hanging, electric, gas ovens?"

"No. I mean it doesn't stop crime."

"In China it is one hundred percent effective," he declared merrily. "The executed never commit another crime."

We had reached the pagoda, tiered, sunbaked and insignificant-looking. The judge pumped my hand.

"A great pleasure," he said. He waved towards a building beyond the trees. "Come to my court. We are very efficient." He made the chopping motion. "Everything very correct."

He mounted his bicycle and rode off with a wave, his gruesome trophy gazing back at me, its tongue flapping as the bicycle bumped over flagstones.

I sat on the steps of the pagoda. Birds chattered in the upper storeys. The place retained some atmosphere of academia. I felt if I listened hard enough I could still catch the scratching of quills. For Chinese Buddhists the task of translation was mammoth; there are 1,662 works in the canon. For Kumarajiva the work was a necessity, not a joy. Reading sutras in translation, he once said, was like eating rice already chewed by someone else.

So arcane is the process of purchasing train tickets in China that many Chinese depend on *guanxi,* the well-developed network of contacts, friends and family, through which so much is secured in China, from a job to a wife. Only the poor, the hopelessly unconnected, and the foreign are to be found queuing in the booking office, pathetic mugs who don't know any better.

Train tickets are the Chinese Holy Grail and their acquisition has a religious flavour. The ticket windows mimic the confessional with wooden doors shooting open and shut over small dark screens. With the windows placed at waist height, you are obliged either to bow or to kneel as you approach. The supplicant posture, the air of mystery, the adherence to ritual and the correct form of words, the belief that the shadowy figure beyond the screen might intercede, might grant absolution, if one could only find the right formula—the whole heady mix is Catholicism at its most obscure.

The scene in the Wuwei train station was depressingly familiar. A cobwebbed queue of petitioners stood before two closed ticket windows. I settled down to wait. Someone handed round a flask of tea.

When I eventually reached the window, and made my request for a ticket to Jiuquan for the following day, I was met by the squeak of rejection familiar to any visitor to China. *"Meiyou,* she said, without lifting her head. *Meiyou* is the eternal negative. It chimes through Chinese days marking shortages, red tape, and laziness.

I asked about the next day. *" Meiyou."* And the day after. *" Meiyou. "* I asked about the next week. *"Meiyou. "* The next month *"Meiyou. "* I became insistent, asking for a ticket for Jiuquan on any day within the next ten years. The little door slammed shut.

I returned three days running to be met with the same denials. Trains came through Wuwei every day heading west to Jiuquan and points beyond but, if the ticket office could be believed, they arrived and departed full. There were no tickets, ever.

At my hotel I offered the staff large sums of money to procure tickets by fair means or foul. I promised to bribe whoever needed bribing. But they only shook their heads sadly. There were some things even money could not buy.

I decided to try to get arrested so the authorities would run me out of town. Camera in hand, I went in search of military subjects. I photographed two army jeeps in the main street. I photographed the railway station, a bridge, the court-house, the gaol and the Public Security Bureau headquarters. I photographed the radio mast from three different angles. I had enough stuff for a full-scale invasion, but no one took any notice. Finally I went back to my hotel and photographed the army officers lounging in the lobby. Far from protesting, they posed happily for a group portrait and invited me to dinner. I refused on the grounds that I was a Russian spy. They laughed heartily and slapped me on the back.

The next day I played my final card. I went back to the railway station, and asked to clerk to marry me.

"Where to?" she asked.

"Nowhere. I am asking you to marry me," I said.

She looked up, a minor triumph in itself. I could see her struggling for words but even *"meiyou"* would not come.

"I want you to marry me." I spoke loudly. I sensed an audience would be useful. The queue awoke and pressed forward, intrigued by this novel approach. I could see other staff emerging from back rooms. This was something more than a weekend return to Lanzhou.

"I can't get out of this town so I have decided to settle here. You are the only woman I know. I want you to be my wife."

The stationmaster had arrived, hitherto a reclusive figure.

"Sir," I said, warming to my role, "I wish to ask for the hand of one of your employees." I had spent the previous evening swotting up my Chinese, abandoning the chapter entitled "At the Railway Station" for the higher ground of "Visiting friends" and "Formalities."

Called from his nap, the stationmaster was dishevelled and confused. Had he been more alert he might have adopted the usual procedure of closing the ticket window. Still bleary from sleep he faltered, and asked me what the problem was.

"I cannot buy a ticket," I cried. "So I must have a wife."

Behind me the queue, astonished to find the stationmaster among them, were growing agitated. In a moment they would all be wanting wives.

Marriage proposals have a way of concentrating minds. The station-master and the clerks retreated into the back room. A moment later my prospective fiancée reappeared and shoved a ticket to Jiuquan through the hatch before slamming it shut. I lifted it like a trophy. The queue gazed at me dumbstruck then broke into a little ripple of applause. Faith was a fine thing, and theirs had been reborn.

Six

THE LAST GATE UNDER HEAVEN

If China has been isolated historically, geography is partly to blame. To the east and the south lie the South China Sea and the Pacific Ocean. To the north lie the Gobi desert and Siberia. West lie two of Asia's greatest barriers: the Tibetan plateau, rising to the Himalayas, and the Taklamakan desert, the great dead heart of Central Asia. That Chinese mythologies peopled these regions with imaginary devils is hardly surprising to anyone who has traversed them.

The bolt-hole that allowed the Journey to the West was the Hexi or Gansu corridor, a long panhandle stretching north-west from the Yellow River for a thousand miles. Squeezed between the Qilian Shan, the snow-capped ramparts of Tibet, and the drifting sands of the Gobi it is reduced in places to a passage less than ten miles wide. This was China's back door, the route taken by Zhang Qian in pursuit of the Heavenly Horses and the route followed by Marco Polo 1,500 years later. For western caravans, trekking along the Silk Road between fly-blown oases, it was an inauspicious approach to the Celestial Kingdom. For the departing Chinese, the bleak landscapes, the backward people, the dust storms and the bad roads confirmed their worst fears.

Faced with the same natural obstacles, the modern road and the railway to Xinjiang still cling to this tenuous passage. Along its length one watches China unravelling. The population thins and the farmhouses are walled like fortresses. Gravel flood-beds break through the fields of haycocks and sheep with nagging regularity. Some are as wide as lakes, and we crossed the dry beds on low causeways. In the spring they carry the spate of the Qilian Mountains to an early death in the Gobi.

In this frontier region the population has a history of disloyalty. Originally Gansu was the territory of the Xiongnu, the nomad tribes whose border incursions prompted the quest for horses. The Chinese eventually pushed them westward where their conquests led, under Attila, to the invasion of Gaul and the siege of Rome. Gansu is now largely Chinese but Hui, Chinese Muslims, their religion a legacy of the road. Their loyalty too has been suspect. As recently as the 1930s the Hui joined with their fellow Muslims in Xinjiang in a revolt that made a bloody chaos of these western territories for the best part of a decade.

Given that the ticket had almost cost me my bachelordom, I was surprised to find the train half empty. The carriages were as underpopulated as the landscape. The explanation was ridiculously simple. This was the milk train, a slow creature that stopped at every bush. I had not known of its existence and only the threat of marriage encouraged the ticket clerk to suggest it as an alternative.

I dozed by the window in the hot sun, stretched out in unaccustomed space. When I awoke fields and meadows were melting into the desert. The Qilian Mountains loomed out of a pewter haze, stern and comfortless. Freight trains trundled past packed with water-melons, heading back east, stirring the desert floor and covering us with another layer of dust.

In these wastes the stations were often the only buildings, self-perpetuating outposts, surrounded by tents, green for the army, white for the railway workers. At one a barefoot soldier emerged blinking in the midday sun, scratching himself, his hair still tousled from sleep. He stared at the passing train as if it was part of his dream.

The passengers were the people of these outposts. Two young women sat opposite in drab blouses. One polished her nails with a hairbrush while the other leafed through a fashion magazine. On its cover was a glossy model, her sweater falling off one shoulder, but inside the glamour vanished on pages of brown industrial paper crowded with muddy print. A soldier and a railway worker came along the carriage and sat down brazenly to chat them up. It seemed a sign of how far we had come from the refined manners of the metropolitan east. Sadly, the two sexes found they had little to say to one another and the encounter soon degenerated into card games.

In mid afternoon when I came back from making tea at the samovar we were suddenly amongst fields of mustard and sunflowers. A breeze silvered the poplars and the mountains were blue with cloud shadows. Horses grazed in water meadows. Two greys, startled by the train, wheeled and galloped away, their tails flying. We were passing Shandon, on the edge of the old imperial grasslands that stretched south towards the mountains. During the Sui Dynasty, early in the seventh century, 100,000 horses bearing the emperor's brand were pastured here. To the north amongst the tangle of hills I could see ramparts of the Great Wall shadowing our route westward.

By day's end the Gobi had returned and rain began. The horizons vanished and the desert was full of sad puddles as the day petered out in damp twilight.

All day the train had grown emptier. It felt like the train to nowhere, gradually abandoned by its passengers. Lying on my bunk I could hear disembodied whispers carried down the strange acoustics of the empty carriage. We stopped somewhere and I could hear singing from outside the window, a soft female serenade. But when I cupped my hands to the glass and gazed out through my own blurred reflection I could see nothing but a single street-lamp in the darkness, its pool of light full of rain.

* * *

Jiuquan was a small country station and I was the only passenger to disembark. The booking hall was empty save for a few passengers wrapped in their coats asleep on the benches. The clock said midnight. I crossed to the main entrance and looked out on a long straight road stretching away into the darkness in the direction of the town. It was clear there would be no transport at this hour.

The rain came on, driving across the road in slanting gusts. I retreated to the station and settled down to join the sleeping forms on the benches. There I might have passed a quiet night had I been Chinese. But as I was making up my bed with sweaters for blankets and my shoes for a pillow, a soldier appeared.

He was a boy lost in an army greatcoat, his hair sticking out beneath his cap. He dismissed my sleeping plans with a wave of his hand and led me along a corridor to a luxurious waiting room of sofas and deep armchairs. For a glorious moment I thought I was to be allowed to sleep here among the inviting cushions.

The only inhabitants of this room were three women in the uniforms of train attendants. They sat with their feet up on the chairs. Their caps lay in a row on a coffee table. They were the sergeant-majors of hard sleeper, whiling away the hours between trains.

The boy soldier, having deposited me in a chair, looked back and forth between the three like a puppy dropping a stick at its master's feet. Had he a tail, he would have wagged it. Had they biscuits, they would have thrown him one.

The three women turned their gaze from the boy to me. They looked as welcoming as prison guards.

"Who are you?" one asked.

"A passenger," I confessed foolishly.

The one near the window snorted with laughter, then coughed up a great ball of phlegm which she deposited in a spittoon at her feet.

"Where are you from?"

"From England," I said. "By way of Wuwei."

"Where are you going?"

"To sleep," I said.

"It is forbidden to sleep in the railway station," barked the one by the window in her best sergeant-major voice.

"I'll just stand around until morning then," I said. I turned to go. There didn't seem much chance of a sofa.

"You must use the baggage check-in," the first one barked.

"It's okay. I'll keep the bag with me."

"No. No. You must check it." The boy soldier, their enforcer, had stood up.

"All right, all right. I'll check it."

As the boy showed me out the three attendants smiled malevolently at each other. Along the hallway the boy knocked loudly on a door, then vanished in the direction of the booking hall. As he did so, a woman shrieked and the door flew open. In the dark room stood a Chinese Fury. A mass of wild hair framed a livid face. My first impression was of a cornered animal who had turned on her pursuers. But when she found only a confused foreign devil the anger abated, and the Fury retreated into a mask of two shining eyes. She backed into the room, and I lumbered in after her with my bag.

"I am sorry to wake you," I said.

"You didn't. They did." She jerked her head toward the attendants' room at the end of the corridor. "They hate me."

"They didn't think much of me either," I said.

The woman began filling in a baggage form. Against the far wall was a mass of radio equipment and a microphone. Against the other walls were metal racks filled with ticketed items of luggage. One of the bottom shelves was strewn with blankets, the baggage woman's bed, a steel shelf without a mattress. She lifted my bag and tossed it onto an upper shelf with the ease of a weight-lifter.

"That's why they sent you here," she said. "To wake me, to disturb me. I hate them. They are barbarians." Her eyes shone. The Fury was re-emerging from behind the mask.

"I'll let you get back to sleep," I said, backing towards the door. "I am sorry about all this."

Suddenly the Fury became the hostess. "Have some tea. You must be tired. Sit down. Please."

I sat down. I was tired. The journey had been all right but arrival was proving rather wearing. At the window the woman tugged at the blinds, then crossed the room and locked the door. I had given up wondering what was going on.

"I am so happy you have come," she said suddenly. She poured the tea like a schoolgirl playing at grown-ups. "It becomes so lonely here." She sat back cradling her mug. "Do you live in Paris?"

"London," I said.

"The same," she sighed. "Is it *too* beautiful?"

"Only in parts. Chiefly the parts I don't live in."

"It must be busy. Arrivals and departures. Here no one comes. The train puts down only townspeople. Never any strangers."

"What's so special about strangers?"

"Without strangers everything is the same," she whined. "I like strangers. I am always looking for them."

It occurred to me that I was part of a prepared script. I was the Stranger who arrives one day by train to set stories in motion.

"Are you the announcer as well?" I asked, motioning to the radio equipment, hoping to divert the conversation.

"I am the station broadcaster," she said self-importantly. Broadcasts were ubiquitous in China. Every train, every boat, every town seemed to have its own disc jockeys broadcasting good news, weather and exhortations to responsible citizenship over public address systems. It was a kind of talking muzak, part of China's ghastly communality.

She sensed my distaste. "I wanted to be an actress. I trained in Beijing. They were happy days." She looked round the small room. "I don't belong here. That's why they hate me. It is envy. They spread gossip about me."

"Gossip?"

"They say I have two husbands."

"I see."

"They are ignorant people. Why should I live like them?" The remark seemed to leave the question of bigamy unresolved.

"Did you marry in your home province?" I asked.

She nodded. "Jiangsu," she said, conjuring a landscape of rice paddies and canals and grey-tiled roofs. "I wanted to audition for the Jiangsu Song and Dance Ensemble. But I was from a bad class background." She cocked her head as if listening for sounds from the corridor. "What did they say about me?"

"They didn't mention you."

She seemed disappointed. "They are devious," she said, as if silence was another kind of gossip. "They say I sleep with the train drivers." She made a noise, a low growl that swelled in her throat. It seemed to release demons, and her mood lightened again.

"More tea?" She fussed with a thermos and tea-leaves. "Do you like my blouse?" she asked suddenly. It looked like the kind of frilly hairdo that women went in for at the court of Louis Quatorze. She clapped her hands. "We must dance."

She hurried across the room to the radio equipment and shoved a cassette into a player. When the music began, the pedantic ballroom dance music of China, she turned it up as loud as it would go. "Come," she cried, holding her arms out. Her grip was like a wrestler's. I had the feeling that at any moment she was going to throw me for a hold. The music was loud enough to be audible all through the sleeping station. She waltzed me powerfully about the room. When we reached the end of the number I thought freedom was at hand but she started immediately into a two-step, kicking my reluctant feet into the correct positions. We went on like this for a good half-hour. The tango was a particular ordeal. I closed my eyes and thought of England while she threw me about the room like a rag doll. On the slower numbers she got me into a kind of headlock. I wondered if everyone who checked their bags at Jiuquan had to go through this. I had a vision of the three train attendants listening outside the door, snickering.

After a particularly vicious foxtrot she fell onto her bunk laughing. "We are made for dancing," she sighed. In a moment she was asleep, snoring like a train.

In the end I slept against the wall in a corner of her room, no doubt further inflaming the gossip mill. Shortly after dawn I left the announcer broadcasting the martial music that the Chinese so enjoy at an early hour, and got a lift into town in a coal truck. In a street near the Bell Tower I found a hotel, a delightful place where sparrows flew up and down the hallways between the potted ferns and the overstuffed armchairs. Then I went out and gatecrashed a wedding.

I was looking for lunch and had wandered into a promising-looking restaurant. The place was packed and meals were being distributed with a panache not normally associated with the Chinese catering trade. A bespectacled man bore down on me and pumped my hand. I took him for an enthusiastic manager. He gave me a buttonhole and took me to meet his bride.

Any hope of a quick bowl of noodles had to be abandoned. The wedding party was in full swing and I was quickly installed as the guest of honour. People queued to shake my hand. I was seated at the head table and a consort produced. She looked like a young Madam Mao, complete with prison haircut and Buddy Holly spectacles. She turned out to be the local Party Secretary. When she smiled the room darkened.

The happy couple had been married that morning in the romantic surroundings of the local police station. In a nation mired in bureaucracy, it was fitting that the ceremony had consisted chiefly of filling in forms. The groom proudly produced the marriage papers for my inspection. Preserved inside a plastic folder embossed with a red star, they consisted of their photographs and personal details, rather like a joint bus pass. Handed round respectfully from guest to guest, the bus pass enjoyed the place of honour reserved in western festivities for the wedding cake

The couple's progress towards true love had been a bureaucratic steeplechase. As Party cadres they would have sought the permission of their local branch, *tan nian ai*, "to talk about love," a deterrent rather like having to ask permission of a girl's father before kissing her. Engagement required the agreement of the Party and their work unit. In order to live together as a married couple adjustments were necessary to their residence permits. When they decided to have a child they would again apply to their work unit. Finally a rigorous system of economic disincentives would restrict them to one child, in line with government policy.

It was no wonder that the wedding party seemed so determined to have a good time. The barking numbers game—a numerical variant of paper, scissors and stone—had broken out at most tables and the reception had begun to sound like an auctioneers' convention. Having shaken my hand the entire wedding party now joined another queue to drink toasts with me. Such was their enthusiasm that I began to suspect the existence of an admonitory Chinese proverb: He who does not drink toast with foreigner at wedding party courts misfortune.

The chosen firewater was an eye-popping rice spirit like a mixture of antifreeze and Liebfraumilch. This being a wedding, the usual egg-cup was deemed insufficiently celebratory. Three egg-cupfuls of white lightning was the bare minimum for each toast. Anything less would have imposed a severe strain on Sino–British friendship. I did my duty, a burden which became progressively easier. By the time the third cousins reached me, things were going swimmingly.

The food arrived too late to save me. Chopsticks were suddenly as manageable as a couple of strands of spaghetti, a difficulty not helped by the fact that my table companions could not take their eyes off me. Opposite was a fat girl unable to stop giggling long enough to eat. I appeared to be the sole cause of her merriment. On my right were a clutch of rumpled chain-smoking nephews who, believing the young couple had been doing more than talking about love, were taking bets on a child arriving before nine months were up. The odds were attractive, 7–2, on.

In the opposite direction two sisters with narrow teeth, high Mongolian cheekbones and matching red sweaters questioned me closely about my personal life. I seem to remember I made most of it up: a wife tragically killed in a ballooning accident, children at a boarding school in the Argentine, a family estate given over to weeds and poachers. I was having a wonderful time.

A new round of toasts was breaking out, this time with the bride's mother. Guests hurried across the room to her with raised glasses. She was a small woman in a brown cardigan and a knitted hat. Slightly flustered, she stood up for her toasts, tossing back her egg-cups with little giggles. The effect was dramatic. Before our eyes mother-in-law became slatternly, a creature of appetites. She leant on the groom's father, massaging his shoulder suggestively.

My consort, Madame Mao the Party Secretary, took this opportunity to ask me about the Great British Revolt of 1984. Bewildered, I said I must have missed it. At any rate there hadn't been any mention of it in the *Guardian*.

It turned out she meant the miners' strike. Comrade Scar Girl, she declared, was a Great Peasant Leader. Did I think I could convey the fraternal greetings of the Central Committee of the Gansu Communist Party to Comrade Scar Girl? I assured her I would speak to the Great Helmsman personally, assuming of course the authorities had been foolish enough to allow him the continued freedom of the streets.

The speeches had begun. The keynote address had been entrusted to the groom's father, happy to escape the clutches of mother-in-law. An erratic character, he veered unpredictably between theatricality and fumbling shyness. The Party Secretary translated his thick country accent. He was a farmer and he took as his theme the husbandry of livestock, littering his speech with what seemed rather unsuitable farmyard analogies. It was received in silence. Next to him mother-in-law, smiling benignly, looked in danger of sliding into her soup.

All in all it was a jolly party. I went back to my hotel and slept for twenty-four hours.

Chen Yi's clothes gave him away. He was dressed in a well-tailored navy blue Mao suit. It identified him as a Party Official but also marked him as a provincial, set apart from metropolitan political circles, where the Mao suit seemed to have been superseded by a job lot from C&A. In a nation where much political debate is allusive, a person's dress is not to be overlooked.

I met Chen Yi in the lobby of my hotel where we had both paused to watch a James Bond film on the television, its broadcast a mark of the dramatic changes in China through the 1990s. In a casino as glittering as Versailles, 007 was surfing through waves of fat men and *décolletée* women. It was a world as alien as the moon. Chen looked at the film as my father might have done, with an expression of bemusement and injury.

I was relieved to meet Chen. He was a sincere and upright figure in a nation that seemed to have surrendered to cynicism and corruption. A loyal Party cadre, he was wrestling with the contradictions of economic liberalization. He had been a young man at the time of Liberation, and the changes seemed an abandonment of the Party's hopes and principles.

"The idealism is gone," he admitted upstairs in another lobby where we had tea. "Now we are left dealing with practicalities unguided by principles."

He seemed happy, almost eager, to speak to me. It allowed him, I suppose, a rare frankness. I asked if he agreed with the economic reforms and if he felt the Party would ever reverse them.

"No, we will not reverse them," he said without hesitation. "We cannot afford to. They are the engine for growth. We live in an era of rising expectations. State control could not provide the growth we need. And politically the reforms have proved too popular to reverse."

"I agree with the changes only because we have no alternative. But I am disappointed. The reforms have benefited the cities and the coastal regions enormously. But here in Gansu we see little of the benefit. The people here are very poor and they are becoming poorer. They are the people for whom the revolution was made, and we have failed them."

"But even they agree with the changes," I said.

"They agree because change promises much. But it will only deliver to the few. We failed them because we did not convince them. Communism is a kind of religion, not just an economic system. It is not enough to change the means of production. You have to change people's hearts as well. We failed to do that. Perhaps we were foolish to believe we could. People are as they are, and always will be. Perhaps we were guilty of seeing the world as we would like it to be, rather than as it is. That is a failure of youth."

Years of campaigns culminating in the disaster of the Cultural Revolution had exhausted people's interest in politics, and discredited idealism. In 1978 the Third Plenum issued a call "To Seek Truth From Facts," in other words to see the world as it is. The ideals of self-sacrifice and service were replaced by the new ethos of the "Open Door" and "Getting Rich First." The drift from idealism to pragmatism is as much a feature of a nation's life as of an individual's. In people of Chen's generation, the two were poignantly combined.

Like most Party members Chen Yi spoke with great reverence of Yan'an, a remote town in north Shaanxi, the end of the Long March, where the Party leadership sought sanctuary in the difficult years between 1936 and 1947. Here Mao, Zhou Enlai, Deng Xiaoping, and the other Party leaders had lived simply and co-operatively according to the Communist principles they were soon to try to reproduce across a nation of a billion people. That the idealism and camaraderie of Yan'an should have arisen from the ashes of old China, backward, feudal, cynical, is a triumph of the human spirit. That they should have led eventually to the Cultural Revolution is salutary.

"Human nature," Chen said, "was a far more formidable opponent than international capital."

I had stopped in Jiuquan in order to visit Yingda, the village where Fu Wen had grown up. I think I hoped the place would offer some connection to her. At any rate I would know that most intimate of things— the landscape of her childhood.

I hired a bicycle and rode into the countryside. Moored between sheep and grazing horses, the road was full of sunlight and bicycles trailing blue shadows and meandering donkey carts, their drivers dozing amid muddy turnips. It was a landscape recovering from rain. The wind rattled the leaves of the poplars along the road and the ditches were sodden. In single-track villages, ending abruptly in cabbage fields, carts were mired in mud and peasants in boots plodded between low square cottages with stacks of hay on their roofs. The day smelt of animal dung and cut wheat and newly-turned earth. Tall clouds rode past a line of birches towards the snow peaks of the Qilian Shan.

On this sunlit road I was thrilled by a sense of freedom, far from the crowds and the scrutiny of China. All those things which must have oppressed Fu Wen excited me: the fields of cloddish earth, the endless skies, the long bicycle ride, the mud, the cabbages, the distant trees faint as smoke. I saw space where she had seen emptiness. I was thrilled that I hadn't seen a car all morning. I remembered how she had loved the treat of riding in taxis in Xi'an. Mine may have been the facile pleasure of the traveller—I did not have to live here—but it was my reward for the habit of departure.

Yingda was a line of two-storey buildings along the main road, housing a row of shops. They sold the staples: rope, inner tubes, cigarettes, bottles of firewater and shovels. There was a shuttered post office and a dilapidated township hall, like a boarded-up dance-hall. Below the road was a duck pond. A man in a straw hat, fishing, appeared to be asleep, and in danger of falling in.

In the square I met a doctor, a soldier, a nurse and a mid-wife. They were out for an afternoon stroll and invited me home for tea. We repaired to the room that the nurse and midwife shared in a small hospital below the duck pond. It was a cement cell softened by crochet mats, sentimental pictures cut from magazines and the trailing gossamer draperies of their mosquito nets.

The nurse and the midwife were Cheer and Gloom, as inseparable as Yin and Yang. The midwife sat on the edge of her bed plucking moodily at the cover while the nurse, all bustle and activity, found seats and made tea. The midwife was responsible for the pictures of sad-looking horses, dewy-eyed children and sunsets, while the nurse dealt in crochet and sympathy. As ever, Gloom was the more alluring.

The soldier was attired in the kind of greatcoat in which Napoleon's army had perished on its way to Moscow. It gave him a romantic air. The doctor, a tall intense young man, had long tapering fingers and lank hair swept forward in the manner of Roman senators.

The nurse served tea and the kind of biscuits on which horses lunched. The soldier, an irrepressible sort, ate four. Our meeting had a certain poignancy for him.

"I am glad we meet in happy circumstances," he said. "For years I have been practising to kill you," he held up an imaginary gun. "Bang, bang," he cried. The midwife thought this was hilarious. She lifted her head to a photograph of the Lake District pinned above her pillow, and rocked with silent depressed merriment.

Later I went on the doctor's rounds with him. There were only five patients in the small hospital, all women, and all suffering, according to the doctor, from abdominal pains. They were on drips while happily munching sunflower seeds and spitting the shells onto their pillows. One of them, a rather wild old woman, lifted her shirt to reveal withered breasts, and pleaded with me to examine her. The doctor stepped in and probed her stomach with his long medical fingers.

"Abdominal pains," he concluded after some thought.

The last of the five women had abdominal pains of a most dramatic sort. Crouching on her bed on all fours, she howled at the ceiling. She was in labour. Her mother and sister were in attendance while the chain-smoking husband loitered sheepishly against a wall, rather overwhelmed by events. He seemed to feel my arrival was a good omen and rushed forward to press cigarettes on me, brushing aside my protestations that I didn't smoke. His enthusiasm was such that I feared he was going to ask me to be godfather. He cut a rather pathetic figure, like a gatecrasher hoping no one would notice or object to his presence. When the midwife arrived, he hid in a closet where he was betrayed by cigarette smoke leaking under the door.

The doctor's accommodation made the nurses' room look gay and palatial. Narrow as a cupboard, it contained a cot, a table, a cardboard suitcase and a white coat hanging on a nail. I assumed he had just arrived, had hardly unpacked, but it emerged he had been there for eight months. It was his first appointment from medical college in Lanzhou. He was an acupuncturist. He showed me his needles which he kept under his pillow in a green velvet case, holding each of them up until they glinted in the light.

The doctor had an evangelical enthusiasm for traditional Chinese medicine. There seemed to be nothing it could not cure. Much of the suffering in western society, from heart disease to impotence, appeared to be largely unnecessary, awaiting only the introduction of well-chosen panaceas from the East. He waxed lyrical about snake's gall-bladder, extract of deer's tail, ground lizard skin, essence of frog, caterpillar fungus, anteater scales, and ox penis, finely ground. Macbeth's witches began to sound like cutting edge of modern medical science.

As if to confirm my worst fears, he produced a geomancer's chart from beneath his pillow. It was an octagonal arrangement of sectioned concentric spheres, densely populated with symbols and characters. It portrayed nothing less than the entire Universe, in some intricate balance of physical and metaphysical elements. The acupuncturist used it for determining the most propitious time for treatment. It was also useful for determining the site of your parents' graves, the correct orientation of the marital bed, and where you should place the new latrines.

This primitive geomancy is the oldest form of Chinese philosophical impulse, dating from the time of the I Ching, thousands of years before Confucius. It mixes the wildly esoteric with the mundane, and is notable for giving free rein to the dreariest of Chinese preoccupations—the need to categorize, to list, to number. In China nothing seems to exits until it has found a category. The division of every element of the universe into either Yin or Yang was only the beginning of this bureaucratic madness.

Numbering is its most meaningless expression. No modern political campaign has stood a chance without a number. The Party passes resolution affirming the Four Cardinal Points. The Red Guards dedicated themselves to smashing the Four Olds, observing the Eight Antis, and rooting out the Black Five. Public health campaigns concentrated civic minds on the Four Pests (sparrows, mosquitoes, fleas, rats). Social programmes encouraged the Five Talks (politeness, civility, morality, social order, and hygiene) and the

Four Beauties (language, behaviour, heart, and environment). Matrimonial success, which used to depend on finding a husband who could supply the Three Runnings (watch, sewing machine, bicycle), has now graduated to the Three Bigs (refrigerator, cassette player, television) while the urban élite have moved on to the Eight Bigs (television, refrigerator, stereo, camera, furniture, washing machine, motorcycle, and electric fan).

Everything seems to acquire existence as part of a group. In China, one is the loneliest number.

In the late afternoon, the doctor and I went for a walk, following the raised banks of the irrigation canals across the fields. At the duck pond the fisherman had vanished. I thought for a moment I saw him floating belly-up in the green water, but it was only a dead dog. The doctor enthused about the fish to be had from this watery graveyard and then, like a man remarking on a common wildflower, pointed out a herb trampled along the edge of the path that was the cure for AIDS and another that cured cancer. These breakthroughs in medical research left me so breathless I neglected to pick samples.

The day was drawing to a close. Banners of light hung between the ragged clouds while dusk was already sidling through the trees. I thought of Fu Wen, reminiscing about her childhood, her mind full of the landscape that I now stole across, unseen.

A little girl came skipping after us. She was a flurry of bony limbs, tugging at our hands, scampering ahead of us until it seemed it was she who was leading us through the landscape. As we passed she called to field-workers who grinned up at her—a familiar figure, this thin wraith dancing along the raised causeways. For a time she seemed to vanish beyond a screen of poplars, only to re-emerge laughing through corridors of corn.

She led us to water meadows by a river where horses grazed on lawns of green light. All at once they lifted their heads as if someone spoke. One by one they began to walk towards us, towards the girl, their tails flicking. They approached with widened nostrils, savouring our scent, their great heads bobbing suddenly as if they were bridled. The girl delved in her pockets for apples. Snuffling into her palms for the fruit, the horses stood around us in the falling light like warm monuments, their breath smelling of grass, their steaming flanks quivering with delight and anxiety. The girl had forgotten us. We were excluded from this ritual of apples. A silken rump swung round and jostled me aside. We backed away, almost guiltily, as if we had stumbled upon some secret, a forgotten ceremony of innocence: a circle of horses, creatures of worship, attendant on a child. We left them in the fallen twilight indulging their appetites.

I took a bus to Jiayuguan, wheezing across a stony desert where lines of new saplings were dying of exposure. To the south, leaden clouds melted down the flanks of the mountains.

The town of Jiayuguan seemed to have misplaced its past. The grid of wide boulevards offered only shoddy apartment blocks, municipal buildings and factories. The shops were tiled like public conveniences. A large population of students, rootless in pink dormitories, had inherited an orphan town.

But Jiayuguan is an ancient place, and for China a significant one. In the desert to the west lies the Last Gate Under Heaven, marking the end of the Great Wall and the beginning of the barbarian lands beyond. I cycled out on the pot-holed highway on a rusty Flying Pigeon hired from the hotel gatekeeper. Army lorries trundled to the west chased by spirals of dust. Bent into the wind I struggled across a plain of fist-sized stones and up a gravel track to the gate standing on a ridge. For miles the desert was as empty and as vast as the sky.

The Impregnable Gate is a large fortress of arched gateways and watchtowers. Above the dun-coloured walls three traditional Chinese pavilions perch like exotic birds with plumage of scarlet columns and decorated beams and upturned eaves. For centuries the same pavilions have sat confidently at the entrance to countless Chinese cities. But here on the edge of the Gobi, set above battlements, they looked vulnerable. They marked the end of China.

From the ramparts one can see the Great Wall curving across the desert. It has come two thousand miles from the Pacific to this, its last bastion. A couple of miles beyond the gate it founders and falls into a river gorge, its mission complete. It was never a very effective system of defence. The nomadic hordes whom it was meant to keep at bay had a disconcerting habit of riding round it. But in the Chinese mind the Wall defined some great psychological boundary, between light and darkness, order and chaos, home and exile. Like the man on the train from Xi'an, they speak of Jiayuguan as the mouth of China, and of those lands beyond as "outside the mouth." On this place were concentrated all the anxieties of passages.

It was a lonely spot. To the south were the Qilian Shan, their russet flanks mantled with snow. To the north were the black crumpled faces of the Horse's Mare Mountains. Between these banks the desert ran towards China like a prehistoric river, desolate, wind-struck, and barren. To any Chinese returning from beyond, exhausted by the dry reaches of Central Asia, these Ming pavilions must have been the most welcome of sights, the gates of the Celestial Kingdom. To the departing traveller they were the last echo of China, reverberating down the empty length of the Gansu corridor to die in these desolate marches.

The first such traveller may have been Lao-tzu, the philosopher who inspired Taoism. In the sixth century BC, disillusioned that no one listened to him, he rode his black buffalo through this pass into oblivion. Two and a half millennia later, the zealotry of the Cultural Revolution, which made education and independent thought a crime, sent thousands of his fellow intellectuals in his wake to the oblivion of the labour camps of Xinjiang. In

the long centuries between, a stream of disgraced mandarins, colonial officials, condemned prisoners and political exiles passed this way. On the bricks
of the portals they carved their distress, lines quoted from the Book of Odes,
sad classical verses of departure and exile. All conducted the solemn ritual of
throwing a stone against the western walls. If it rebounded they would return home safely. If not, they would die among strangers and demons.

I followed the Great Wall across the desert to its end. In these regions
it was a crumbling adobe bulwark, its feet buried in drifts of sand. Solitary
hoopoes danced along the ruined battlements. Wild chives flowered in purple profusion on its leeward side. The thin air was laced with the smell of
juniper. In the distance camels grazed thoughtfully on scrub. The railway
pierced the ramparts and a steam train shrieked through the Wall, bound
for Urumqi, the capital of Xinjiang.

I arrived back at the fortress with the last of the light. A red sun, idling
on the lip of the horizon, lit up the western face of the gateway. The red pillars shone, the roof tiles were glazed with auburn light, and the stone face
of the fortress was the colour of pomegranates. Then in a moment the sun
tipped away to the west. The light died and the western face of the gateway
was flat, grey, and dismal.

When I turned away I found I was not alone. A Mongolian, emerging
from behind a boulder, greeted me here on the edge of the Gobi as if I had
arrived by appointment. "Ah, it's you," he said. He wore the battered trilby
hat to which Mongolian men are so partial. With his old baggy suit and
his spectacles, he seemed cast as one of the sad comics of silent films, an
Everyman wrestling with arbitrary fate. Around his neck hung an ancient
box camera.

"You are a traveller?" my new friend asked.

I nodded.

"I am one of these as well," he said. He made it sound as if he was trying to please me.

"Where have you come from?" I asked.

"From the borders of Siberia where the men ride reindeer."

"And where are you travelling to?"

"London," he announced. He seemed to have come the long way round. His eyes swam behind thick lenses. "I am a photographer. Would you pose please?"

He stood me in front of the Last Gate Under Heaven and backed away, stumbling on the stones. His camera looked like it was last used to photograph the Tsar's visit to Ulan Bator. He peered through the view-finder, aiming the camera some way to my left. I edged my way round into shot.

When my portrait was taken he came forward to shake my hand rather formally. I had to guide him towards me by speaking.

"When do you hope to reach London?" I asked.

"It is difficult to say. I am unfamiliar with the road." I wondered if he meant the Silk Road or the A2. "I must go now," he said. "It's getting on. Goodbye and may your road be straight."

With that he wandered off across the plain northward towards the Horse's Mare Mountains. So far as I knew there was nothing in that di-rection for miles, perhaps hundreds of miles. Certainly it wasn't the way to London.

"The road is this way," I called, gesturing towards the highway which lay below us.

He peered back at me for a moment, trying to make me out.

"Ah, yes." Turning and tripping over a boulder, he made his way un-certainly toward the sound of trucks.

"See you in London," he called.

He was the most mysterious man I have ever met, and I fully expect him to appear one day from behind a telephone booth in the Charing Cross Road with that casual greeting, "Ah, it's you."

Seven

THE FRONTIERS OF TARTARY

As recently as the 1930s travellers on the road west from Jiayuguan were greeted with an antique road sign, a stone tablet with a single line of characters: "Earth's Greatest Barrier." It referred to the deserts ahead, the great dead heart of Asia, which stretched well over a thousand miles westwards to the Pamirs. These deserts were the central fact of the Silk Road.

The bus to Dunhuang rattled through a gap in the Great Wall, past the Last Gate Under Heaven, into a landscape of stones. I gazed out at a world of horizontals. The road seemed to be careering into nothingness. Away to the south, the Qilian Shan looked as substantial as a mirage.

For a time the road followed the railway, until the latter veered away behind a line of dunes and disappeared. Presently we came to a fork, marked by a couple of dry thorn bushes. The road that seemed to have no destination was suddenly offering a choice. We turned south. On the map I traced the northern road, the thinnest of lines trailing across a buff-coloured blank towards the Mongolian border. It could be days before you realized you had taken the wrong turning.

Next to me a demented child in a military uniform stood on his seat twirling a pearl-handled toy gun like a pint-sized General Patton. His mother looked exhausted. The general barked orders and his hat fell over his eyes. Looking for enemies he found me and pumped three shots into the side of my head. I feigned a dramatic demise. Later when I ignored the gunshots and tried to read, the general grew fretful. Deprived of his body-count, he began to sob and eventually fall asleep in his mother's lap, sucking on the barrel of his gun.

The landscape was enlivened when the road joined the Shula river which came down from the Tibetan plateau beyond the Qilian Shan. The river was low, its water the colour of the desert. The far bank was fitfully irrigated and the thin slopes of green and the undulating trees were a vision of paradise from the hot bus. Like all the rivers in this part of the world, the Shula was destined to expire in desert, the sea still a continent away.

From time to time beacon towers appeared along the road, ribs of timber rafters showing through their sides. They were the lighthouses of the Silk Road, built over a millennium ago. Using fires, messages could be sent back to the imperial court, a thousand miles to the east, in a matter of hours. Later we passed the ruins of Qiaowan, built by a Qing emperor late in the seventeenth century. The gate of the city had been left ajar and sand filled the streets.

At midday we reached Anxi which geographers say stands at the very centre of Asia, half-way between the Urals and the South China Sea and between the Arctic Circle and the tip of India. It is the Piccadilly Circus of the Gobi. From here desert tracks lead north to Mongolia, south to Tibet, east to China and west to Turkestan.

In an eating-house I squatted at a low table over noodles and feverish flies. Outside in the shimmering street lines of donkey-carts stood along the kerb loaded with fat yellow melons. The farmers squatting in the shade munched on their produce, throwing the skins to the panting donkeys. Beyond them the general was defecating in the gutter attended by mother. Passing trucks stirred the heat and laid thin blankets of dust over the town.

In the afternoon as we approached Dunhuang the desert was littered with graves: cairns of stones and clusters of sticks adorned with coloured rags. At this hour the gravel wastes were full of mirage, and the rag banners of these funeral mounds floated on silver seas. When I lifted my eyes from this kingdom of exile the oasis was capturing the horizon, its trees paddling in shade.

Dunhuang, a remote outpost a thousand miles from anything resembling a city, was a surprisingly sophisticated place. In the evenings the main boulevard was taken over by a café society that brought an unexpectedly Parisian air to the Gobi. At pavement tables beneath the trees one sipped flowered tea or cold beer while watching the promenading crowds and enjoying the first cool breaths of night. Cooks ferried lidded bowls of beef stew to the table from kerbside stalls. Tinny music played from speakers in the trees while farm-workers strolled past hand in hand.

After dinner I went to a dance in a yard at the back of the cinema. Strings of coloured lights had been draped over a cement yard between a derelict bus and the upper windows of a warehouse. Music was provided by a sedate trio of a trombonist, a keyboard player, and a drummer who bounced on her seat like a wind-up toy.

My experience with the baggage handler at Jiuquan had done nothing to dent my enthusiasm for Chinese dances. They were perversely compelling. The music was always the same, formulaic, demure and reliably rhythmic. It was music by numbers and its stilted manner gave even the jolliest of tunes a melancholy air. The dancing, always western ballroom dancing, was in the same mould: correct but rather lifeless. Beneath the sad strings of lights the dancers gazed over each other's shoulders, rarely speaking. It was a triumph of Chinese restraint.

The lack of romance made for a high degree of participation. At Chinese dances, everyone danced. When you did not manage to step out with a member of the opposite sex, you danced with your own, men as well as women. The armed forces were well represented, and soldiers dancing together in their green uniforms and black slippers made fetching couples. The only exception was a group of young farmers who had come in from an outlying oasis. With their patched Mao jackets, their flat caps and their big hands, they looked on hungrily from the shadows, desperate for wives.

My own card was marked by the Fred Astaire of the evening, a grey-haired military man. His uniform was weighted with enough brass to put a rear-admiral to shame. He favoured the stiff arm, the straight back, and the sudden tangoesque turn. It seemed churlish to refuse him. We struggled briefly for the lead but I soon surrendered as he waltzed me away through the throng. The high crown of his peaked cap came up to the middle of my chest.

At 11:30 precisely the band struck up a catchy tune that signalled the end of the evening. The dancers turned like commuters and filed obediently through the gate. Within two minutes the coloured lights had been turned off and the place was empty.

The next day I visited one of the world's leading art galleries. In the hills to the west of the town are the Mogao Caves, the repository for some of the finest works of Buddhist art.

For centuries historians were happy to believe that Chinese Central Asia was an historical as well as a geographical blank. It was perceived as a route between civilizations, its desert soils too poor to allow culture to put down proper roots.

The first indication that the region had secrets to reveal came in the closing decades of the nineteenth century when explorers like Sven Hedin and Colonel Prejevalsky began to penetrate the high passes from the south and the west. Their reports of temples of "Buddhist idols" and lost cities engulfed in desert sands prompted an unseemly scramble for antiquities among

European scholars. In the early years of this century, archaeologists from Germany, France, Russia, Japan and Britain fell over one another in their rush to stake out claims to the various sites. Taking advantage of the remote position of these sites and the loose control of the Chinese authorities, they loaded caravan after caravan with manuscripts, relics and frescos stripped from the walls of cave temples, all bound for the museums of Europe.

These artefacts revealed a remarkable Silk Road civilization, hitherto unknown and unsuspected. Not since Nineveh had there been such extraordinary discoveries. "Here," wrote Albert von le Coq, the German explorer, "a New Land was found." Archaeologists identified it as a Buddhist culture that had flourished until the tenth century. As a product of the Silk Road, it was a hybrid, what Sir Aurel Stein was to call Serindian, a synthesis of the traditions of China with those of the lands to the west—India, Persia and the Hellenized Gandharan cultures of the Indus valley.

The spectacular wall paintings that decorate the cave temples, shrines and monks' cells at Dunhuang are the greatest legacy of this lost civilization.

Something about Buddhism prompted its more devout adherents to a troglodyte existence. From Bamiyan in Afghanistan to Hangzhou in eastern China, the rock faces of Asia are pockmarked with their incessant excavations. Wherever they paused along the Silk Road, Buddhist monks, as persistent as mice, began to burrow.

At Dunhuang, between the fourth and the tenth centuries, they carved more than a thousand caves out of the soft limestone cliffs. Almost half remain, their walls densely adorned with wonderful frescos. The size of the complex and the richness of its artwork identify the site as a popular place of pilgrimage, a Central Asian Lourdes.

The entrance-ways to the cliff shrines were reached from elevated boardwalks. I paused at each threshold to allow my eyes to adjust to the caves swimming out of their gloom after the hard light of the desert. It was the hesitation of a frontier, between the blank expanse of the Gobi and the crowded and magical kingdom of the monks.

Dense lush landscapes fill the shrines. In one cave there is an exquisite spring dawn, a cold blue stream, a hint of blossom on the box trees. Elsewhere beneath ceilings of grapes and pomegranates mountains rise from the clouds. A group of women with beehive hairdos listens politely to Buddha in a grove of trees. The King of Khotan, wearing a very complicated hat, poses for a family portrait. Wildcats mix happily with human-headed birds. Musicians and tumblers perform while a man holding a lotus rides past on a white ox. Horses with neatly-tied tails parade under the gaze of a dragon sprawled across a ceiling. Bands of decoration run round the door jambs and invade whole rooms, a riot of repetition. The colours are still strident, unfaded in this dry environment and protected from the bleaching of the light outside—malachite green, azurite blue, orpiment yellow, earth red, cinnabar vermilion, kaolin white and lamp black.

Serene and invulnerable, the Buddhas are aloof masters. The bodhisattvas have more charm, deep in thought, one elegant leg crossed over the other, their chins resting pensively on a hand, handsome figures with long fingers and beautifully curved lips. The patrons who paid for the decoration of the shrines to ease their way to Paradise appear in the earliest caves as small supplicant figures. But by the Tang dynasty, a dynamic period in China and the golden age of the Silk Road, such modesty had been cast aside. The Tang patrons stride through their caves like the masters they believed themselves to be, tall figures in rich gowns with their elegant high-waisted wives. There is no point in paying the bill if no one knows who you are.

The Western Paradise is a recurrent theme. In places it looks remarkably like Venice, all canals and *palazzi*. Elsewhere it is a garden landscape full of open-sided pavilions, tiled pools, temples nesting in clouds and duck ponds where fat babies float on lotus leaves. But the dominant motifs of Dunhuang are the flying apsaras, Buddhist angels who sail through the caves from darkness to light trailing silks and metaphors. They reminded me of the horses of Chinese art and mythology, in flight from confinement. Later, in the Dunhuang museum I saw a bas-relief from Yangguan Pass, the Jade Gate on the southern arm of the Silk Road. It showed a horse galloping, fleet as a hare, its legs outstretched, its tail flying, trailing a scarf of silk—an equestrian angel bounding westward into a new land.

On the road back to town one passes the tall ornate stupa that marks the grave of Wang Yuanlu. Wang was an itinerant monk who in the last years of the nineteenth century, finding the Mogao Caves neglected and ruinous, decided to devote his life to their restoration. He is famous today for inadvertently selling the first printed book.

In March of 1907 Sir Aurel Stein, one of the greatest archaeological explorers of these regions, arrived at Dunhuang, having crossed the desert from Kashgar in search of antiquities. Rumours had been circulating in Central Asia about the discovery of a great cache of ancient manuscripts at Dunhuang, and Stein was determined to acquire some of them.

Careful not to reveal the extent of his interest lest it alarm Wang, Stein set about the delicate task of persuading him to allow an examination of the manuscripts. It was not easy. Wang was "a queer person, extremely shy and nervous." Jealous of his authority, he proved "difficult to handle."

In the end Stein was able to win his confidence through the medium of Xuan Zang, the great Silk Road traveller who had brought Buddhist scriptures from India. Stein and Wang shared an enthusiasm for Xuan, and over discussions about his epic journey a mutual regard developed. Eventually Wang agreed to show Stein a few samples of the ancient scrolls. When it emerged that the samples were translations done by Xuan himself of sutras brought from India, Stein was able to portray this to the pious priest as an omen, a sign from beyond the grave that Stein, an admirer come from India, should be allowed to see the entire collection.

The priest set about dismantling the wall he had built to guard his treasures and Stein was soon peering into the closed chamber, in a scene reminiscent of Howard Carter at the tomb of Tutankhamun. "Heaped up in layers," he wrote, "there appeared in the dim light of the priest's little lamp a solid mass of manuscript bundles rising to a height of nearly ten feet, and filling, as subsequent measurement showed, close to 500 cubic feet." It was an extraordinary collection of materials, all of them over a thousand years old, in Chinese, Sanskrit, Sogdian, Tibetan, Runic-Turki and Uighur, as well as numerous unknown languages. Their quantity and rarity made them invaluable to scholars. It was like discovering the Pergamum library.

At first Stein was only allowed to examine the manuscripts. But gradually he was able to persuade Wang to part with some in exchange for a contribution to the shrines. In the end the lure of gold rather overwhelmed the poor priest and Stein eventually carted off twenty-four cases of manuscripts as well as five more filled with paintings, embroideries and art relics, in exchange for a donation of £130. Among them was the famous scroll known as the Diamond Sutra, now displayed in the British Museum, which is the earliest printed "book," produced well over a thousand years ago. The hoard was, in the words of Sir Leonard Woolley, the discoverer of Ur, "an unparalleled archaeological scoop." The *Times Literary Supplement* declared that "Few more wonderful discoveries have been made by archaeologists." The Chinese had another description. They called it piracy. A Chinese history of printing, published in 1961, says the theft of the Diamond Sutra still causes people "to gnash their teeth in bitter hatred."

In China buses always seem to leave at dawn, and my journeys, now that I had abandoned the train line, began in quiet streets among the rituals of sweeping. At this hour, departure had the air of flight. I felt I was stealing away before my hosts were properly awake. In the pre-dawn the road-sweepers were already at work shifting yesterday's dust. Plump mysterious figures in padded jackets and white masks, they waded through the gloom wielding long brooms in somnambulant slow-motion. Cold constellations were falling between the trees and beyond the jumble of dark roofs, roosters were crowing. This was the traveller's dream, to depart unnoticed, unencumbered by farewells, while the sweepers followed in one's wake obliterating footprints.

In the seat in front of me sat three young women, asleep on one another's shoulders, their long glossy hair trailing over the back of the seat and into my lap. I thought of Fu Wen, and wondered if she too was still asleep, a thousand miles to the east, at the other end of this road. I pictured her beneath a white sheet, curled like a sapling, dreaming of strange landscapes. In these stolen departures I through of her waving from the walls of Xi'an. She was a comfort against the lack of farewells. I wondered how she remembered me, in what light, and at what moments. I wondered how long it would be before she no longer thought of me.

Liuyuan was a railway town. When the line to Urumqi was built in the late Fifties, an incrustation of forlorn buildings grew up around the desert station on a single treeless street. Half the population was transient, holed up in cheap hotels, waiting for train tickets or trucks to Tibet. By the look of them, some had been there for months.

In this limbo between arrival and departure people fell prey to mysterious illnesses, and medicine men had descended on the place from the Tibetan plateau like vultures. On blankets on street corners they displayed their wares—strange roots, leaves of unidentifiable plants, animal bones, skulls, hooves, scraps of hide. Customers hovered round the edges of the blankets, wary men for whom waiting had become a way of life. The bravest discussed their complaints in monosyllables. The Tibetans, mesmeric figures in wool capes and sombreros, were assured propagandists. There was nothing their collections could not cure.

After Liuyuan the asphalt ran out, and the bus lurched and jolted on broken tracks. The desert had lost its patina of scrub and stretched away now on all sides as a blank and desolate plain. In this void, the tracks wandered aimlessly, as if unsure of their way, as if the emptiness of this place had sown doubts about their destination.

A madman had boarded the bus at Liuyuan, perhaps one of those deranged by waiting. He wandered up and down the aisle arguing stubbornly with himself. Suddenly he recognized his stop. The driver drew up and the madman got down in the middle of nowhere, marching purposefully away into oblivion with his little bag.

In the Chinese mind these deserts are inhabited by demons. Stories abound of voices calling from beyond the sand dunes, like sirens. Marco Polo wrote of spirits "talking in such a way that they seem to be [the traveller's] companions," sometimes even hailing him by name. Travellers who turn off the track to respond are never seen again. When the siren voices don't work the desert djinns resort to the *kara-buran* or black hurricane, "like hell let loose" in the words of von le Coq. Day becomes night as whirling clouds of sand and stones descend with gale force on travellers. Whole caravans are lost in the confusion and panic of these storms. It was, wrote Xuan Zang rather too confidently, "all the work of evil spirits."

At midday dark outcrops of rock arose ahead of us, their heights commanded by ruined forts. A ravine cut between them. Scattered along its floor were derelict buildings. A couple of eating-houses survived with menus of Chinese characters scrawled on boards outside their doors. There was a petrol pump set in an oily yard and an administrative building behind iron gates. Set apart was an army encampment, a row of dusty tents and a tank with a missing turret, its back to the cliff, a memento of more turbulent times.

This place was the frontier post of Xingxingxia, the Ravine of Baboons. It marked the beginning of Turkestan, of Tartary, now the Autonomous Region of Xinjiang, a province over three times the size of France.

The bus stopped to let two soldiers down. They unloaded sacks of melons from the roof, indecently ripe in this bony place. With the engine off, we could hear the wind howling at the windows. The soldiers' comrades came over from the tents and scuffled playfully with them by way of greeting while all the men got down from the bus to urinate in the sand like dogs marking territory.

Then we drove on into further desolation.

Xinjiang has been Chinese territory intermittently for two thousand years without ever becoming Chinese. Its confused identity is reflected in the wealth of names it has borne at different times in different mouths: Tartary, High Tartary, Sinkiang, Chinese Turkestan, Serindia, Chinese Central Asia. Xinjiang, a Chinese word meaning the "New Dominions," is an appellation invented after a nationalist revolt in the nineteenth century prompted the Chinese to consider naming the regions which they had long taken for granted. In earlier times it was simply the Western Regions. For centuries Chinese control of the area was either indirect or nominal. In weak dynasties they retreated from Xinjiang altogether. Their concern was to maintain it as a buffer. "If Xinjiang is lost, Mongolia is indefensible and Beijing is vulnerable" is one of the older maxims of Chinese geopolitics.

Xinjiang could hardly be more inaccessible. Until recent times, travellers set off for Chinese Turkestan with the same sense of foreboding with which they embarked for Central Africa. It is enclosed on three sides by some of the world's highest mountains: the Tien Shan, the Mountains of Heaven, to the north, the Pamirs and the Hundu Kush to the west, and the Karakorams and the Kunlun Shan, the ramparts of the Tibetan plateau, to the south. Its eastern approaches are blocked by the Gobi desert, stretching a thousand miles into Mongolia.

At its heart lies an even more desolate wasteland, the Taklamakan desert, whose name bears its own warning. It is a local Uighur word meaning "you go in but you do not come out." Maps portray it as an eloquent egg-shaped blank. With the mountains that surround it, the Taklamakan provides the Silk Road with its greatest obstacle. As if hedging its bets, the road divides, branching to the north and the south of the desert, keeping to the oases along its rim. In sight of the great snow peaks that frame the province, the oases are watered by rivers whose destiny is not the sea but a slow death in the grip of the Taklamakan.

The scattered population of Xinjiang is a mosaic of Turkic Muslim peoples, in custom and manner more akin to their Middle Eastern cousins than to the Han Chinese. Their appearance reflects a complex history. Some bear oriental features reminding one that their origins are in Outer Mongolia. Others look like Turks one would meet in the villages of Anatolia. The Turks began migrating westwards from these regions in the sixth century, and Turkish and Uighur are really dialects of the same language.

The Uighurs are the largest group in Xinjiang, the oasis dwellers, the middlemen of the Silk Road. Kazaks, Kirghiz and Tadjiks are nomadic peoples who migrate in the mountains surrounding the Taklamakan, the people who dwell, according to the Chinese, in "a moving country."

The peoples of Xinjiang offer a striking contrast to their Chinese rulers. Where the Chinese cherish order and conformity, the Uighurs are free-wheeling hedonists. Chinese society is one of constraints and responsibilities, the Uighur is more impulsive, more individualistic, more expressive. If the undeclared hero of the Chinese world is the scholar, living a life of reflection and retreat, his counterpart in Turkestan is the traveller or the merchant or even the bandit, canny, willful, unpredictable, and mischievous.

As in other ethnic areas, like Tibet and Inner Mongolia, the Communists have promoted Chinese settlement in Xinjiang on a vast scale. "A good comrade is one who is eager to go where the difficulties are greatest," Mao declared. Endless "Production and Construction Corps" were sent west enticed by higher wages. Labour camps brought more Chinese as Xinjiang became China's gulag. In 1954 the Han Chinese numbered only half a million, about ten percent of Xinjiang's population. Today they are nearly six million, almost half the population. In Urumqi, the capital, the Chinese are now the majority, in the same way that they are in Lhasa. For all the cant about cultural diversity, these massive settlement programmes have been an insidious way of making different ethnic groups, often opposed to Chinese rule, a minority in their own lands.

In a campaign launched in 1963 the Party exhorted the faithful to "Learn from Lei Fang." Apparently he was a young worker who had been crushed by a truck the previous year, though the more cynical believe he was merely an invention of the Politburo. His diary, fortuitously discovered after his death, revealed a model comrade, and he was held up to the youth of China as an example to be emulated—his picture stared down from walls everywhere and his sayings were quoted *ad nauseam*. "A man's usefulness to the revolutionary cause is like a screw in a machine," Lei Fang wrote. "Though a screw is small, its use is beyond measure. I want to be a screw."

Lei Fang is less likely to crop up in Party literature these days, indeed he has become something of a figure of ridicule in modernizing circles. But there is something inherently Chinese about him. He is not just a Communist ideal. He touches upon the ancient Confucian view of the individual as part of a complex whole to which he owes obligations and deference.

I don't know how the Lei Fang campaign went down in Xinjiang. But in these vast landscapes, amongst a restless and untamed people, it cannot have been to the Party's advantage to push this obliging figure too hard. It is difficult to imagine the Kazak tribesman, in tall boots and outlandish hat, a dagger in his belt, astride his horse in the Mountains of Heaven, declaring, "I want to be a screw."

Eight

THE KING OF THE GOBI

The last King of Hami, the King of the Gobi, lived in a palace well stocked with Russian liqueurs and French champagne. In his gardens peacocks paraded between mulberry trees and lotus ponds. The rooms were adorned with silk carpets, cheap paraffin lamps, Ming vases and cuckoo-clocks. In one of the reception halls hung scrolls of calligraphy, gifts from the Empress Dowager in the Forbidden City in Beijing. In the long circuitous passages one might meet a mad nephew, a concubine in emerald silks or the king's Hungarian doctor, a tall aristocratic man in riding breeches and a waxed moustache. Every day the rising and the setting of the sun was greeted with a cacophony of drums and trumpets by the palace musicians stationed on the roof-top.

Maksud Shah, a vassal of the Chinese emperor, claimed descent from Genghis Khan. He was an intelligent and affable man. As well as his native Uighur he spoke both Mandarin and Manchurian. His hospitality was legendary, if at times somewhat inebriated. When he was entertaining the German archaeologist Albert von le Coq, in 1904, no fewer than eighty melons were sampled at table to find one suitable to be presented to his guest. After the melons the banquet degenerated into an endless series of toasts. The king, von le Coq reported somewhat ruefully, seemed quite hardened against the ill effects of alcohol.

Maksud walked a careful tightrope with his Chinese overlords. When he died in 1930, all hell broke loose.

In Hami I went to visit his grave. Maksud was buried with his ancestors in a tomb with a view of Tien Shan, the Mountains of Heaven. It stands on the edge of the oasis where the last poplars are overtaken by sand. I found it one evening, lapped round with shadows. The guardian, a bespectacled old man, was squatting by a wall, drawing Chinese characters in the dust like a schoolboy at his lessons.

There are two tombs and a mosque, the last a tawdry building of debased traditions. In a gloom cut by thick shafts of light, amid a forest of columns, I found a jeep and an old bus. The mosque, which had not yet been restored to use after the depredations of the Cultural Revolution, still doubled as a garage. The old man read the dusty inscriptions round the walls—in Persian and Turki—each prefaced with the opening line of the Koran, *Bismillahi rahmani rahim,* "In the Name of Allah, the Compassionate, the Merciful."

One of the tombs was an unhappy Sino-Islamic hybrid with small domes lost in a Chinese roof of soaring eaves. The other, a domed mausoleum, was magnificent, even in its semi-ruinous state. It belonged to the great Central Asian tradition of Islamic architecture, the first truly Islamic monument I had encountered on the Silk Road. Its architectural antecedents stood in Samarkand, Herat, and the great cities of Persia, a thousand miles to the west. The tall portal was of exquisite proportions, grand, inviting, celestial. Nothing so clearly marked the frontier I had crossed. I had the sense of standing, here on the edge of the Gobi, on the threshold of a new culture, a great tradition that stretched as far as the Atlantic Ocean and the Moorish monuments of Spain.

In the interior where the dome soared in an atmosphere of dust and pigeon dung, the floor was crowded with stone sarcophagi like badly parked cars. Most had been smashed open. The Red Guards, the old custodian said. I bent down. They exhaled breaths of cold stone. When I peered inside I could see nothing, as if the Kings of Hami had been one step ahead of their pursuers.

The guardian locked the gates as I was leaving and we walked together with our bicycles back toward the town. It was sheep rush-hour and the lanes were crowded with hot ill-tempered flocks on their way home from a hard day at pasture. I looked back from time to time at the dome clinging to the last of the light, framed by poplars.

The old man was delighted with my enthusiasm. I asked if many people came to visit it. No one, he replied morosely.

"Who remembers the Kings of Hami now? The Chinese have taken over everything."

The great-granddaughter of the last King of Hami was waiting for me the next morning in the lobby of my hotel. Through a contact in Beijing I had an introduction, and when I telephoned her at her office—she worked for the provincial government—to arrange to meet she suggested an excursion to Barkol in the Kazak pastures in the Tien Shan. Her English was good, delivered in a voice as coarse as sandpaper. She said she would arrange the necessary permits, as the area was usually closed to foreigners.

Artursan was a tall young woman whose dress hung on her bony frame like a coat on a peg. She seemed to be all elbows and sharp shoulders. High cheekbones, wary eyes and a raw mouth gave her face the emblematic quality of a mask. Her manner managed to be both haughty and vulnerable. She had arrived with a bag of sewing, embroidery and bits of lacework, and a little box of sweetmeats. Niyaz, the driver, was an adolescent forty-year-old.

He backed into a tree in the yard of the hotel, shouted friendly abuse at the gardener and we were off.

Artursan sat in the front with Niyaz, donning a pair of rimless spectacles for her sewing. I lounged in the back and for a time the car was silent. In the desert, the road ran like a drawn line between boulders and ruined watch-towers. Ahead the Mountains of Heaven were blue as porcelain, their summits frosted with snow. We rose through a steep valley where yurts, round nomad tents, were bedded into the slopes amongst the pine trees. Wrapped in bedraggled layers of felt, they looked like tramps huddled against the cold. At this early hour gangs of children were out among the flocks of sheep, milking. From the doorways of the yurts, women in white wimples and baggy pantaloons waved as we passed, blue alpine flowers eddying about their feet.

At the top of the pass we got out into a gale of wind. The northern slopes fell away steeply at our feet to a vast yellow sea of pasture on which floated the black specks of Kazak tents and flocks. The wind and the view made us giddy as children, and suddenly we were laughing and joking like old friends. We shouted into the gale. Artursan, thin as paper, clung to a tree. Niyaz flapped his arms and leaned over the precipice.

Back in the car we plunged down a switchback road through glades of sunlight and sheep. "The Russians built this road," Artursan said over her shoulder. "When they were on good terms with the Chinese. It runs to-wards the old Soviet border. They thought it might come in handy one day for invasion."

At the bottom of the pass a Chinese security agent pushed his way through a crowd to ask for my permit. Artursan waved it imperiously at him without giving him time to read it. In this street of Kazaks and Uighurs, he did not feel able to protest. Whatever invisible boundary we had crossed, it had tipped the balance of power away from the Chinese.

We stopped by a stream of elevens. Artursan opened the box of sweet-meats and handed them round while Niyaz produced melons from the boot

1. The end of China, Jiayuguan

2. Ferryman,
Yangtze tributary

3. An echo of the
Silk Road, Muslim
gentleman, Xi'an

4. Backstage at
the Opera, Xi'an

5. Retirement,
Shanghai

6. Nomads, Barkol, the Mountains of Heaven

7. Three Wise Men, Kuqa

8. Refuge, the Emin Minaret, Turfan

9. Test-riding, Horse Market, Kashgar

10. Evening serenade, Ili

11. Wedding guests, Karakul

12. The Lingerie Department, Kashgar Bazaar

13. The Chinese-Pakistan border, Karakoram Highway, 15,528 feet

14. Cart park, Kashgar Bazaar

15. Homeward bound

of the car and sliced them with a dagger. Hami melons, as yellow as lemons, are famous throughout China. Shipments of melons were sent east every year to the Imperial Court in Beijing. We dangled our feet in the water gurgling over a bed of white stones. The melons were sweet as grapes and the air tasted of meadows.

We discussed marriage. Marco Polo had written of the merry wives of Hami, then known as Qomul, who entertained strangers with the connivance of their husbands. "The husband goes out and stays somewhere else for two or three days, and the stranger remains with his wife . . . and is much comforted. And the women are fine and merry and much taken with this custom."

Niyaz was enthusiastic, provided he got to play the stranger and his own wife wasn't involved. He took a happily hypocritical line on marriage. His wife was married but he was still single, he explained helpfully. "All the beautiful womens," he sighed. "It is too much to resist."

"Don't listen to him," Artursan said. "He is afraid of his wife. She would welcome a stranger after him."

Artursan was firmly opposed to marriage, in spite of the fact that her own wedding was scheduled for the following week. She was twenty-six, dangerously old in Uighur society, and familial pressure had been brought to bear. She described her husband as a fat man who worked in a bank, and treated the impending wedding as if it was a hairdresser's appointment she was thinking of canceling.

"I don't know." She shrugged and made a face. "Maybe I won't marry." Given the elaborate nature of Uighur ceremonies, it seemed a bit late for second thoughts. As we spoke relatives were travelling from distant corners of Xinjiang. A new house had been built, dowries exchanged, and sheep slaughtered.

She was rather hoping her fiancé would not expect a traditional wife. This seemed a trifle ambitious. Until very recently a man's status in Xinjiang was measured first by the number of his sheep and second by the number of his wives. It was a Muslim society where obedience was the only female virtue.

"Come away with me," Niyaz said, picking his teeth with his dagger. "I will be your lover. We will all run away together to Inglistan. I will be Mr. Stanley's driver in London."

She had almost gone to England, she said. She had read English literature at the University of Urumqi and there had been a scholarship to enable a student to study for a year at Cambridge. She had applied. She was one of the best students, in spite of the fact that tertiary education is in Chinese. But the award had gone to a Chinese girl—a poor student according to Artursan—whose father was a "big potato" in one of the provincial Ministries.

"This is the Chinese," she said wearily. "They help themselves. You might think in Xinjiang such a scholarship should go to a Uighur student. But no, the Chinese take them." She spat with sudden ferocity. "We are sick of these Chinese."

The experience seemed to represented some defining moment in her life. Bitterness lay about her like a shawl. The unwanted marriage seemed an act of surrender, a way of confirming her anger and disappointment.

We had lunch in a Kazak yurt spread with wine-coloured carpets. Felt mats, gold and sky-blue, climbed the walls. We sat cross-legged with our backs to tiers of travelling trunks, as gaudy as amusement booths, and almost as big. A circle of sunlight fell into our laps from the chimney hole in the domed ceiling as we waited for our host.

He arrived with the sound of horse's hooves, and came into the tent bearing a riding crop, like a character in Chinese opera. He seemed to have come from a different climate. Though the day was warm he wore two shirts and a heavy jacket buttoned at the neck. He was a short brusque man with sleepy eyes and cheeks glazed with a patina of broken veins.

News of Hami was exchanged. It was clear that our host saw it as the big city with all its attendant ills. He seemed to view the Uighurs as a disadvantaged people, a people without flocks. I was a further mystery. He asked me how many sons I had, and when I said none he seemed to wonder what I had been doing with my time. Then he asked me how many sheep I owned. I tried to explain that sheep were difficult in a London flat. Rather graciously he did not enquire further, aware that I led the same aberrant sort of life as the Uighurs, a life of towns and houses.

"I own a hundred sheep," he said. "And ten horses." He apologized for his relative poverty, explaining that his parents had both died young.

This modesty about his wealth turned out to be a bargaining ploy. He assumed that I was a travelling salesman. While he answered my enquiries about the summer and winter pastures he was waiting to hear what I had to sell. When he learned that I had come to Barkul only out of curiosity he was bewildered. Here I was, a man without sons or livestock, who came from a place he had never heard of and who had crossed the Gobi on a whim. Artursan rallied to my support but everything she said—that I was a writer, that I had come all the way from Shanghai—only served to confirm his view that he was giving hospitality to an idiot.

A woman brought lunch in a large white sheet, unfolding it to reveal an uninviting mound of hard crusts of bread. Bowls of sour milk, garnished with ash from the fire, were set before each of us. The idea was to soften the bread in the milk until it reached edible consistency.

Later, full of old bread and sour milk, we went outside into the sunshine where two horses had been saddled for us. Our host's eldest son was going to take us towards Barkul. He was a gallant fellow with a scarlet scarf and a romantic's face. A worldly young man, he was able to regard me as acceptable company despite my not being a travelling salesman. He made little enquiry about England or China but was fascinated by the idea that I had been to Dunhuang, which seemed to stand on the furthest limits of his horizons.

Niyaz, who viewed horses as he might a second-hand Lada, was not coming, but Artursan took her saddle with considerable confidence. My own mount was a small black mare who in the course of the afternoon revealed herself to be the Mata Hari of the equine world. Only the firmest hold would keep her from eloping with every stallion whose scent appeared on the afternoon breeze.

We rode over undulating pastures. Distant flocks of sheep drifted round the sloping horizons tended by shepherds on horseback. In this empty steppe people appeared and disappeared as mysteriously as clouds. When we turned our heads we spotted a young girl riding past on a gaily caparisoned horse herding two pack camels. When we looked again she had vanished over a yellow hill. An old man arrived with a small flock of sheep which paused to drink at a stream. He wore a tall astrakhan hat and an overcoat belted with a white silk sash, and was mounted on a leggy stallion. Mata Hari, a martyr to lust, made an exhibition of herself. In the ensuing fracas, the old man and myself were nearly unseated in mid stream.

We rode on through encampments where the nomads greeted us with glasses of fermented milk which we drank in the saddle. It was the best season of the Kazak year, early summer, when the pastures were rich and the flocks fat. At one place a gang of women were making felt, beating the wool with thin bastinados. At another a group of four dignitaries, cross-legged and enjoying the view, sent respectful greetings to my mother and father, as if they knew them. Children called after us shyly and a great flock of herons passed overhead going towards China, their long wings beating with a curious grating sound.

In a grove of pine trees we found Niyaz waiting with the car. The doors were open and he had put on a cassette of Uighur music. The words were all hopelessly romantic, "your eyes, your lips . . . met me tonight in the moonlight . . . I will love you always even when you leave me . . ." In the pine-scented clearing we took turns dancing with Artursan. The Kazak horseman sat on his heels clapping time. When we eventually induced him to join in, he danced solo with much foot-stamping in his tall boots. It reminded me that the word Cossack was a corruption of Kazak.

Later the boy rode away through the trees with our two horses trailing after him. We drove down to the road and followed it back to the pass. In the car, inspired by the songs, I said, "Perhaps marriage without love is a dangerous thing."

Artursan shook her head. "I don't think so. Love is for songs, for adolescents. In marriage it is love that is dangerous. There are too many expectations."

When the old king died in 1930 the Chinese governor of Xinjiang saw it as an opportunity to assert his authority over Hami. He had Maksud's son, Nasir, brought to Urumqi and placed under house arrest. Chinese officials were dispatched to Hami where they embarked upon programmes of tax and land reform that, for all their fine rhetoric, systematically dispossessed Muslims in favour of Chinese settlers. The removal of their political and religious leadership, the theft of their land and the imposition of harsh taxes caused unrest among the Uighurs. But when a Chinese tax collector raped a Uighur girl, it sparked an open revolt.

It was the beginning of a decade of bloodshed in Xinjiang. The local population in Hami turned on the Chinese, massacring civilians and soldiers alike. When Chinese troops were sent to retake the city the atrocities were repeated, this time with Uighur victims. The Kazaks joined their Uighur cousins but they were little match for the well-armed Chinese troops now arriving in considerable numbers. Cornered, the Turki Muslims of Xinjiang appealed to the Chinese Muslims of Gansu, and in particular to the young warlord Ma Chung-yin. Religion proved stronger than race and

Ma Chung-yin made a dramatic dash across the Gobi to lay siege to the Chinese garrison of Hami. It was the start of a campaign in which Ma galloped back and forth across Xinjiang at the head of a marauding band of irregulars, drowning political priorities and national aspirations in an orgy of plunder and blood-letting. *Ma* is the Chinese word for horse, and the little general's nickname was "Big Horse."

It was the end of the horse in Chinese history. The short-lived success of Ma's campaign was dependent upon his mastery of cavalry in the wide spaces of Xinjiang. Eventually it was brought to heel with the weapons of a new age: aeroplanes, armoured cars, and machine-guns.

Sven Hedin, the great Central Asian explorer of the last quarter of the previous century, made his final journey to the region in the midst of this chaos and wrote an account of his experiences in a book entitled *Big Horse's Flight*. Hedin likened him to the Fourth Horseman of the Apocalypse, the rider on a pale horse bringing death and destruction. I thought sadly of the Heavenly Horses, the beautiful creatures of Tang ceramics, and the dancing figure of the Flying Horse in Lanzhou. The old gods, it seemed, were dying.

On the bus to Turfan the luggage racks were full of saddles and the passengers swayed on their seats like horsemen. All day we bumped along the edges of the Taklamakan Desert, through red and black hills dropping occasionally to lakes of blond sand. To our right the peaks of the Tien Shan were shredding clouds. To the left the desert was as bleached as the dry sea bed of some ancient ocean. From the old shores we gazed out over petrified waves. I imagined whale bones and marine fossils but saw only camel thorn dancing in the wind.

At Shanshan where the bus stopped for a few minutes I found a Chinese man panting in the shade, slurping watermelon. He gazed out at the desert with a look of panic, hardly able to believe the ghastliness. He greeted me like a long-lost friend. In these barbarian regions the foreign devil was suddenly an ally.

He was an entymologist sent to Xinjiang by some ministry, presumably the Ministry of Insects, to study a moth whose larvae infest fruit. Though it was a considerable pest in Xinjiang, it had not yet reached "inside the mouth," by which he meant China proper. Some barrier must be created, he muttered. He held his sticky hands up in front of him, conjuring a Great Moth Wall.

After the desert, the smell of trees and water is the sweet smell of paradise. It happens in a moment, in a turn of the head. Suddenly we were spinning down a road lined with poplars, past cornfields and vineyards. Water channels bubbled, lanes were overgrown, and men lay in the shade of old trees with their feet up on cart wheels. We slipped from one world into the next as abruptly as Alice fell into Wonderland. Travel has few delights to match the arrival in a desert oasis. Overcome, a hearty fellow in a pink hat muttered in my ear: "Grapes." The word sounded plump and indecent.

For centuries Turfan was "the bright jewel of the Silk Road," a key staging-post on the road to Cathay. In winter it is the coldest place in China. In summer it is the hottest, so hot it is said you can cook an egg in the sands. It never rains in Turfan and the oasis is supported by a remarkable system of underground channels, known as *karez,* which carry water from the Tien Shan beneath the desert floor to its waiting fields. It is an idea that came from Persia along the Silk Road.

Water is everywhere in Turfan, as silky and seductive as temptation. Away from the ghastly municipal boulevards built by the Chinese, the sound, the sight, the smell of water is inescapable. In roadside canals geese paddle, children play, and women wash bright billows of laundry. Ducking under walls the water flows through every courtyard like a household god. In the streets in the evenings a water-truck lays the dust, a merry vehicle which plays Christmas carols over its speakers. The driver, a bedraggled Santa Claus in a tea-cosy hat, was humming along to "Hark the Herald Angels Sing." It was mid August in the deserts of Central Asia.

Grapes are to Turfan what oranges are to Seville. The famous "mare's nipple" grapes, which were sent to the Imperial Court two thousand years ago packed in snow in lead-lined boxes, still grow in profusion. Trellises shade the courtyard of every house and in some parts of town whole streets are canopied with vines, dappling the donkey carts and the cyclists with a soft light.

The water and the heat and the endless vineyards give Turfan a languorous quality. Its abiding image is the bed. In the hot months people sleep out-of-doors and the beds—large antique wrought-iron constructions—were everywhere, along the roadsides, in the fields and the vineyards, on the flat roofs and in the courtyards, on the pavements and street corners. They were rarely unoccupied, and one tended to tiptoe about the town as whole families slept bundled together like puppies through the midday heat.

This air of indolence can undermine even the most determined travellers. A Dutch family arrived at my hotel bristling with maps and guidebooks and plans. In three days all the vigour of northern Europe had dissolved in an Asiatic lassitude as they lay all day on carpets beneath the trellises, drinking port and reading poetry and cheap thrillers. The mother held out the longest—washing clothes, making enquiries, looking up train schedules—but even she eventually succumbed. When I found her daughter massaging her feet one morning while her husband peeled grapes for her, I knew the façade of industry had fallen.

The Turfan bazaar, in the heart of the old town, might have been at the other end of the Silk Road—Aleppo, Damascus, or Isfahan. Bathed in a ruby light filtering through the coloured awnings which span the lanes, it was crowded with carpets, rolls of silk, coils of rope, saddle-bags, and endless piles of green grapes. The men wore tall boots, long coats, daggers and embroidered caps. Among the women the veil had a modest following. The Uighur fashion in veils is rather makeshift—a small brown blanket thrown over the head so the faithful look like bank robbers being hustled from court past the press photographers. Female modesty, however, does not extend equally to all parts of the body. The women keep their money in the tops of their stockings, and any transaction involves hoisting their skirts to reveal red bloomers and milky thighs. With time I became as familiar with the undergarments of the women of Turfan as I was unfamiliar with their faces.

I was a great hit in the bazaar with a mixture of newly-acquired Uighur laced with a smattering of Turkish half-remembered from a journey through Anatolia. After the difficulties of Mandarin I had taken to Uighur with enthusiasm, swotting up every night. The Uighurs were invariably delighted with my fumbling efforts. The Chinese say "There is no hell like a foreigner speaking Chinese." The Uighurs clap their hands and embrace you. In the bazaar a crowd gathered, eyebrows upraised. Was I from Turkey? they asked. A fellow mussulman from Istanbul? they asked. Flattered, I acquiesced in this pleasant fiction.

White lies are like quicksand. I was soon the talk of the bazaar. Every stallholder wanted to shake my hand, every greybeard wanted to pay his respects. I returned the following day to find the story had grown to unrecognizable proportions. I was a wealthy Turk in need of a wife; I was an Islamic scholar touring the mosques of Xinjiang; I was a great *effendi* looking for long-lost relations. Afraid of exposure, I escaped into frantic rounds of sightseeing.

The lost cities of Central Asia are the ghosts of the Silk Road, unquiet souls, inadequately buried. In these regions where life is always fragile, and climate and fate are equally cruel, the mystery of their deaths remains unsolved. Princes lost their thrones, trade was disrupted, wells dried, the *karez* were blocked, the desert grew capricious—no one can be sure.

Overwhelmed by sand and misfortune the stumps of buildings, smoothed by centuries of wind, hint only obliquely at their past. The found objects more clearly disclose a city's identity—manuscripts, jewellery, coins, cooking pots, clothes that no one bothered to pack, as if the end had come suddenly. In the empty streets where camels were nosing for scrub, it was as if the inhabitants arose one afternoon, a millennium ago, and walked off into the desert.

At the ruins of Gaochang, once the great trading city of Khocho, four German expeditions searched the sands before the First World War like prospectors panning for gold. Sherds of illuminated manuscripts, fragments of silk paintings, bronze figures floated to the surface, cultural flotsam in a dry sea, glinting marvellously. In one season alone von le Coq discovered seventeen different languages in the twenty-four scripts, a roll-call of Asian tongues, all carried here along the Silk Road.

These cities enjoyed a wonderful eclecticism, the imprint of other worlds from the Mediterranean to the South China Seas. There were few orthodoxies here to restrict the appeal of new ideas which arrived with the snorting camels and the exhausted merchants. Just as Khocho became home to the exiles and outcasts of other empires, so it was host to religions and philosophies discredited in their homelands.

Two of the more exotic were Nestorian Christianity and Manichaeism. The Nestorians were hounded out of the Church at the Council of Ephesus in 431 for insisting that Christ was human. In isolation they moved ever eastward and went a bit odd. Priests abandoned celibacy for bigamy. Friday became the holy day and communion often turned into a drinking bout. Genghis Khan was brought up by a Nestorian guardian, which is hardly a thing a religion can boast about.

Manichaeism was a rather mysterious syncretic religion from Persia, persecuted by Muslims and Christians alike, with dualistic views about the equal nature of God and Satan. Between the fifth and the seventh centuries it spread with remarkable speed, its missionaries ranging from northern Spain to Beijing. Persecution brought an equally rapid collapse and in this remote place the faith found one of its last havens. The gorgeous illuminated Manichaean manuscripts that have been unearthed at Khocho are all that remains of what was once a world religion.

My own haven was the Emin Minaret. I liked it so much I retreated to it most afternoons when the bazaar merchants came looking for me, eager to press their daughters on me. I cycled through the shaded back streets where children fought and chased donkey-carts, and women slapped their washing on boulders. The minaret stood beyond the town, its feet in a green sea of vineyards.

The mosques of Turfan tended to be vernacular affairs, jaunty street-corner diversions, painted in pastel greens and pinks, their walls meeting at curious angles, their courtyards adorned with picturesque old men in riding boots. The Emin Minaret, by contrast, is a Great Work which would be an impressive monument anywhere. It belongs to a tradition of minaret building peculiar to Central Asia and eastern Iran where minarets became as spectacular as the Pharos. The Emin Minaret, built in the eighteenth century, is a late-comer. It tapers from a thick base through tiers of herringbone brickwork. Its antecedents are Khusrawgrid, Sangblast, and Ghanza. With a neat symmetry, they in turn are architectural descendants of the watch-towers of the Silk Road whose ruins are still to be seen round the rim of the Taklamakan. These cross-currents make the Emin Minaret a considerable traveller. It has been to Persia, and back.

In the adjoining mosque, a study in white geometry, love-sick pigeons stirred the gloom. Columns and arches receded like a trick of mirrors. It was an exquisite and lonely place where one could write poems in the layered dust.

* * *

No one has every spoken well of Urumqi, and I am unable to break with this miserable tradition. The capital of Xinjiang, it is a dusty congested place of tawdry modernity. All over Xinjiang, Chinese urban planners are destroying traditional Uighur towns with their wide public boulevards, their roundabouts full of marigolds and frightful statues, and their municipal buildings tiled like lavatories. In Urumqi the triumph of Chinese urban planning is complete.

I stayed in a monolithic Soviet-style hotel that seemed to have fallen into the hands of the criminal underworld. Black marketeers filled the lobby, the receptionists seemed to double as prostitutes and the service desk attendants sold soap and towels as if they were stolen goods.

I shared a room with a Pathan from the North-West Frontier. Khusal was one of that growing band of Pakistani traders who are the true heirs of the Silk Road. They cross the passes of the Karakorams to Kashgar then fan out along the old road to trade in what they can carry which, if you are a Pakistani, is considerable. You see them all over Xinjiang, wrestling sacks the size of garden sheds onto the roof-racks of buses.

It was Khusal's first trip to China and he was still in shock. He found the Chinese incomprehensible. "They speak only Chinese," he complained.

"I think they put something in the water," he said. "To keep them quiet. They are like dead people. They look at you as if you are not there." He wrung his hands. "The men," he cried suddenly. "What is the matter with them? In Pakistan when we are seeing a beautiful womens we are getting in a lather. Our hairs are standing up. Here, nothing. The men have died, leaving only their shadows."

Khusal himself was in love with a woman whom he had met on a bus and whose telephone number he had managed to procure. Her name, appropriately, was Ringle. He spent all day trying to ring her. Usually the telephone was answered by Chinese-speakers who, finding him incomprehensible, hung up. Occasionally his beloved Ringle answered.

The lack of any common language made it impossible to arrange a rendezvous but they got on famously over the telephone with the international language of love. Khusal would retreat beneath the blankets with the receiver and for the next hour nothing but a series of muffled coos and giggles emerged.

Afterwards he suffered post-telephonic *triste*. He sat on the bed glumly. "I am alone," he sighed. "And no one understands me."

In Urumqi a good day out is a visit to the dead. Xinjiang is remarkably well blessed with cadavers. The climate suits them. The dry sands, the desert air, preserve them as faithfully as formaldehyde. Former citizens come marching down the centuries in an alarming state of preservation. One can think of living people who don't look half so well.

Mixing with the dead is of course a controversial affair. In Cairo, the pharaohs are no longer receiving visitors; the whole thing was thought too unseemly. No such scruples inhibit the Chinese authorities. Every museum in Xinjiang has its corpses. They are invariably a sensation. One doesn't linger long with old pots and obscure coins when the people who used them are in the next room.

In Urumqi's museum they had a suite of rooms on the upper floor. With low lights it had the ambience of a well-appointed funeral parlour. People lowered their voices and took their hats off. The dead were arrayed about the room, each to their own glass case, their eyes averted from one another, like a family that had quarrelled.

The heads of this clan were an elderly couple still in their dressing gowns. The woman, more than two thousand years old, looked as if she had dozed off in front of the telly, her hands folded across her tummy, her mouth fallen open to reveal four sharp incisors. The old man looked the silent type, a man who would give anything for a quiet life. Death suited him. Among the others was a rather striking young woman, a bit of a flirt with a deep cleavage, her shirt casually unbuttoned to reveal how well preserved she was.

In another case lay a baby swaddled in red cloth and wearing a blue woollen bonnet. There were pebbles on its eyes. A label identified it as "Apparatus for suckling milk—1000 bc."

Nine

HERE BE DRAGONS

Ili teeters precariously on the edge of China. Lying at the far end of a westward arm of the Mountains of Heaven, nearly two thousand miles from Beijing, it is remote even from the rest of Xinjiang. The border of the old Soviet Union is only thirty-five miles away. When the Russians occupied the town in the eighteenth century, Beijing was unaware of the incursion until informed by St Petersburg.

For the Chinese, no disgrace was so complete as banishment to Ili. It was the ultimate exile. Among the stream of sacked officials who were dispatched to this border outpost was Qishan, the Manchu governor who made the mistake of ceding Hong Kong to the British. Ironically, a similar fate awaited Charles Elliot, the British signatory to the treaty. Displeased that he had not secured better terms from the Chinese, Lord Palmerston made him chargé d'affaires in Texas.

The Chinese were not alone in seeking Ili's isolation. Floods of exiles from all over Central Asia have made the town a hotchpotch of dispossessed communities. The professional letter-writers who conduct their business on the pavements outside the post office operate in a dozen languages.

The bus takes two days to reach Ili from Urumqi. The road lies across a plateau of high winds and thin pastures where sheep and horsemen negotiate the long horizons. Towards the end of the second day the bus climbed the slow pass to Saryam Lake in the lap of snowy hills where all the passengers got down to wet their flannels in the glacial waters. The road fell suddenly down the far side of the pass through pine forests to the valley of the Ili river where the horsemen from the hills picked their way through unfamiliar crops.

Russia casts a long shadow here. Everyone I met insisted on speaking Russian to me as if it was the lingua franca of the non-Chinese world. In the back lanes of Ili, the houses have blue walls with shuttered windows and carved *nalichniki* frames. In this remote place they were comfortingly European.

I took a donkey-cart from the bus station to the hotel. The driver was a toothless old fellow who saw himself as the racing demon of the Tien Shan. We took the first turn on one wheel, and I almost toppled out the back. In order to ensure full throttle on the straights the demon jammed a cruel stick into the poor donkey's rectum, a technique which produced astonishing acceleration. Nearly airborne, we flew through the town running over dogs and scattering cyclists. Far ahead I could see pedestrians, familiar with his driving habits, hurtling for cover. Oblivious to all this the demon kept up a babbling monologue over his shoulder. I gathered that he was a single man in possession of a good fortune and in want of a wife.

Ili had a frontier feeling. The streets were full of horsedrawn tarantasses with red awnings and jangling horse-bells. In the municipal avenues sheep were grazing through beds of marigolds. A cinema, set behind a barricade of rubble, broadcast an unending soundtrack of gunfire and agonized groans. Horses were tethered outside the doors of shops, and drunks roamed the streets. They fell off their bicycles, careered into lampposts and were sick on the doorsteps of restaurants, thereby presenting prospective customers with a rather garbled version of the menu.

Inside the gate of Ili Hotel was a bust of Lenin looking anxious. The hotel was built in the Russian style with blue and yellow dachas set amongst birch trees. The lobby of the main building was like a Chekov set, deep brocaded sofas, tall double doors, a dilapidated chandelier, and pine boughs tapping at the windows. The staff were nowhere to be found so I checked myself in to a room with a view of chicken coops and mountains. Later a receptionist came to call. She wanted $100 a night for the room but eventually settled with exemplary good grace for the equivalent of $5.

On my second evening in Ili I had a visitor at my hotel. He sent one of the cleaners to my room with his card, which announced him as Gao Fen, Professsor of Ceramics. Downstairs I found a slight bespectacled man sunk into a corner of one of the sofas.

"Mr. Stanley?" he said, struggling to his feet. "I am a friend of Wang's."

Before I left Shanghai Wang had given me Gao's address and told me to look him up if I was in Ili. The two men had been deported to Xinjiang on the same train in 1967, and had spent five years together in a labour camp in Wusu. From Turfan I had written to Gao to introduce myself and to ask if I might see him.

We sat down, sinking into the cushions. The melancholy scent of dust and old velvet enveloped us. Gao was a frail figure, dwarfed by the sofa. He might have been seventy-five. In this wild place he seemed quintessentially Chinese, reserved, cautious and correct. His eyes floated beneath blue lids. In his lap his long fingers were knotted tightly together.

He was grateful for news of his old friend, still alive, and in good health. But once he had sight of these two essentials, he did not enquire further, as if Wang and Shanghai were now such a distant world it was pointless trying to digest news of them.

"Are you from Shanghai?" I asked.

"Suzhou," he said. It was an ancient city in eastern China, a town synonymous with culture and scholarship. In the old days it was a place to which mandarins retired to lives of contemplation, calligraphy and the classics. They planted the exquisite gardens for which the city is still famous. Suzhou could be a metaphor for the sophistication and refinement of the lands within the Wall.

"What did you do in Suzhou?" I asked.

The hands opened and floated up above his knees, palms upward, long-fingered and empty.

"I was a collector." His voice was a whisper. "I collected porcelain."

During the mania of the Cultural Revolution much of China's artistic heritage was destroyed. Museums and galleries were ransacked and temples were broken up. It was the triumph of barbarism, the very threat that had haunted Chinese civilization for millennia. It came, not from beyond the Great Wall, but from the nation's children, gangs of adolescent Red Guards. The finest Ming vases, priceless scroll paintings, statues of Buddha, were all attacked in the same way as coloured ribbons in a girl's hair or a blouse that was deemed too bourgeois. Artists and connoisseurs suffered with their art. Denounced, beaten and imprisoned, many did not survive. Those that did suffered re-education through labour, many in the gulag of camps scattered across Xinjiang.

Gao recalled the day in the summer of 1966 when he had passed the Paired Garden near his home in Suzhou to find students tearing up the plants, ravaging the spring blossoms as objects of bourgeois pleasure. He had watched them dumbstruck. The banners and the gathering crowds chanting slogans told him that this lunacy was official, or at least as official as anything was in those days. The Party, it appeared, had declared war on flowers.

Gao had lived in one of the old whitewashed houses overlooking Suzhou's canals. The Red Guards descended upon him in his own home, interrogating and haranguing him in shifts night and day, forcing him to write endless self-criticisms and confessions. When he showed insufficient enthusiasm, they beat him. But infinitely worse than these beatings was the destruction of the porcelain.

It was a family collection, passed down through three generations. His great-grandfather, a provincial official, had begun it with some pieces that he purchased in Nanjing, a set of five green glazed jars from the Song Dynasty. Each generation had added to it. It was an heirloom, and the maintenance and appreciation undertaken by each new generation had been part of that very Chinese reverence for one's ancestors. Gao had devoted himself to it, becoming an expert in the periods it best represented.

The Red Guards had forced him to smash the collection himself piece by piece. They threw the sherds into the canal.

Gao spoke slowly as he told me this, as if reliving the shock. He was a reticent man and he had not, he explained, spoken about the destruction of the collection to many people. The memory was too painful for public display, and he could not bear the pointlessness of relating it. Nothing would bring them back. Then too, he said, so many people had lost members of their family, that it was difficult to speak about vases. But he was an old man now. If he died with this tragedy as a secret their triumph would be complete. Now he wanted as many people as possible to know about it.

"They were not strangers, outsiders," he said, his palms pressed together. "They were the children of our neighbourhood. I had watched them growing up. They took pleasure in all this destruction as children take an innocent pleasure in breaking things." His hands unfolded against his shirt front in some gesture of protection. "Youth is a terrible thing. Terrible."

He had been tried as a counter-revolutionary and sent to Xinjiang, where he worked for five years in a coal mine. He was released in 1972. I asked why he had not returned to Suzhou.

"I will never go back to China," he said. "Never."

"Would you not be happier in Suzhou?"

"I cannot go back to live among the people who did this. They are still there, as if nothing had happened. They blame everything on the Gang of Four. But it was not the Gang of Four in my house, smashing my porcelain, beating me with sticks. It was not Madam Mao who was there. It was my neighbours, the children of my neighbours, who did this. Now they say I am free. So I am free to reject them. I prefer to stay here as far from them as it is possible to be."

Gao's exile placed him firmly in a Chinese tradition in which intellectuals, faced with an unpalatable regime, withdrew. Confucius advocated conformity or retreat, a pattern reinforced by the Party's endless campaigns and purges. China entered the twentieth century with a remarkable cultural continuum but almost no tradition of intellectual confrontation. It was unprepared for the revolution of ideas that the modern world would unleash. During the Cultural Revolution there were countless acts of individual kindness towards the victims, often undertaken at considerable risk, but little public opposition. Good people kept their heads down and waited for the pendulum to swing back.

Gao subsided into the sofa. Its ancient dusty odour seemed to have become some emanation of this man, the scent of exhaustion and bitterness. His hands fluttered to his lap and were still. The Cultural Revolution was long over, but rejection had become so much a part of him he found it impossible to see a future without it.

"The ringleader of the Red Guards was a boy from my street," he said. "He had been a delightful child. I can still remember him. His house was on the corner next to the vegetable stalls. He used to play on the doorstep with his sister and when I passed we had a little ritual of greeting. He called me 'big potato,' and I called him 'little potato.' It always made him laugh."

He could not get over the idea that this barbarism, this cruelty had come from the people of his own district, from his own street, from within not without.

Of all the exiled people who have taken root in Ili, saddest perhaps are the small besieged community of Russians who have lived there since the eighteenth century when the town was briefly part of the Tsar's territory. When I asked where I might find them, no one seemed to know of their existence. The Russians kept their heads so low they were virtually invisible.

I found them, after much searching, in a quiet neighbourhood of wooden verandas and door-to-door butter salesmen. I would not have found them at all but for a chance turning where I saw a great blank wall at the end of a street. It appeared to be the remnant of a church, a gable-end with ancient double doors and a little cross still clinging to its eaves. When I pushed the doors open on sagging hinges I found, not a nave, but a yard surrounded by blue Russians houses. I had blundered into a hidden world, sprouting in ecclesiastical ruin. In the middle of the cobblestones stood three children, blond and blue-eyed.

The Russians of Ili where the archetypal ghetto community. For more than two hundred years they had preserved their cultural identity, a tiny isolated island in an alien sea. An ancient treaty had given them fishing rights to a stretch of the Ili river, and from this they eked out a living. Many of China's political upheavals had marked them as suspects and enemies. The Sino-Soviet split of the early Sixties, the Cultural Revolution with its anti-Soviet rhetoric, and the border clashes of the Seventies had all fostered a siege mentality. They had retreated now into the nave of their church, destroyed by the Red Guards, like monks withdrawing to the sanctuary of their abbeys in troubled times. The community numbered only a few hundred, a population that was inevitably dwindling.

The houses were a vision of European domesticity. Lace curtains hung in the windows. Beyond I glimpsed framed pictures, an old clock, lamps with tasselled shades, and an iron bedstead. A man appeared in a doorway in his vest and gazed silently at me with his doleful Slavic face.

He spoke neither Chinese nor Uighur. Here was a fellow European, and yet he was the only person in Ili to whom I could not say hello. I resorted to theatrics, hoping to break the ice. Wondering about the successor to this building, I drew a picture of a church and mimed worship, a performance that emerged as a cross between Jimmy Swaggert and Monty Python. He shook his head sadly, a response that in the circumstances might have meant anything—no church, no chance of seeing it, no understand, or no point playing the fool with me.

A group of children had gathered around us. My audience might not have been very enthusiastic but at least it was growing. I tried to discover if the man was one of the Russian fishermen on the Ili river. I did everything, casting nets, fly-fishing, reeling in a couple of big ones, throwing in a comic turn about the size of the catch, but the circle of faces gazed back at me blankly. I felt like an alternative comedian at a working-men's club in Barnsley.

Finally I tried graves, as if a cemetery might lighten the atmosphere. I drew a series of crosses in the dust. The man looked at me for what seemed an age, then led me round the end of one of the houses past chained dogs and lines of laundry. We walked through the vanished west door and into the old churchyard. Almost lost in the long grass were numerous mounds. Only a few bore headstones. The Cultural Revolution, or perhaps anti-Russian sentiment stirred up by the border clashes, had swept through this cemetery, defaming the dead. There were no dates earlier than 1976, the year of Mao's death and the subsequent arrest of the Gang of Four.

The man hovered nervously at my side as I toured the gravestones, glancing over his shoulder from time to time towards a road visible beyond a low wall. I realized he was anxious that no one should see me here, that the Chinese should not have an excuse to make more accusations against them. Suspicious contact with foreigners was a charge to which they were particularly vulnerable.

I turned to go. In the doorway the Russian declined to shake my hand, but as I left he stepped back into the privacy of the yard and waved, that I should know his refusal was not meant as a personal slight.

In the evening I dined with two drunken Kazaks. They joined me uninvited at a table beneath vines, rolling like sailors in a heavy swell. They had just graduated from the university in Urumqi and the evening debauch was by way of celebration. One disappeared briefly beneath the table and threw up over his friend's shoes, then reappeared smiling like Liberace, keen to reassure me that all was well.

Speech was more or less beyond them. One apparently spoke English. He had a narrow face and flattened hair and looked like a post-orgy Nero. The other, the sick one, was a Russian-speaker who seemed to have come from central casting as a B-movie lead, handsome but seedy, a second-rate Vronsky already happily embarked on the road to ruin.

He poured me a glass of white lightning with its familiar bouquet of paint stripper. He was at the point where he was keen to get rid of the stuff.

Feeling a toast coming on, he stood up suddenly, spilling the drinks, and almost upsetting the table.

"Osman Batur!" Vronsky cried, raising his glass.

Nero leapt to his feet. "Osman Batur!" he chorused.

They tossed back their drinks, wincing. Vronsky sloshed more into our glasses. The table, awash with white lightning, had become a fire hazard.

"Osman Batur," Nero began, carefully taking his seat. "The George Washingtons of Kazak peoples."

"He was from Ili, wasn't he?" I said. I had been sipping my drink like a bar hostess, pouring it on the ground when the Kazaks were looking the other way.

Nero sat back in surprise, almost losing his balance. "You know Osman Batur!" he cried.

"He fought with Big Horse," I said. "With Ma Chung-yin."

Nero slapped his friend on the chest, a thunderous blow. Vronsky took it like a scrum half, steadying himself momentarily on the table. "Famous in Inglistan!" Nero cried.

They shot to their feet again. "Osman Batur!" they bellowed. "Osman Batur!" They were proving tiresome dinner companions.

Cigarettes were then produced and Nero fumbled with matches. When he dropped one into the ponds of liquor the whole table was suddenly alight, an impressive *flambé*. The Chinese owner sprinted out of the restaurant brandishing a meat cleaver and my two companions fled into the darkness.

I found them at the end of the street where Nero was trying to rescue Vronsky from a roadside canal into which he had fallen. Leaving his friend to sink he clasped me to his bosom. "Osman Batur!" he cried. "Tomorrow we go to the mountains. You must come. Riding, dancing, chasing the girls. Tomorrow."

Remarkably, the two Kazaks turned up the next morning at my hotel. They arrived in a horse-drawn tarantass, lying in the back like stone effigies. The driver cracked his whip, the horse bells jingled, and we rattled away between the dachas and the pine trees, past the bust of Lenin and out through the streets of Ili. I had no idea where we were going, but the morning smelt of adventures.

Beyond the town the landscape was full of stubble fields and autumnal orchards. Donkey-carts cluttered the road laden with fruit. We rode through invisible chambers of scent—wood smoke, apples, horse-dung, strawberries, wet grass. The river lay on our right, smoothly swollen sheets of water, green as jade. After a time it fell away, carrying a line of trees towards the frontier. The landscape grew emptier, the crops giving way to pastures. A herd of cows had invaded a graveyard, nosing among the headstones, munching the dried flowers, a cud of old griefs. The houses were mean dwellings with pinched windows and grass invading their flat roofs. They were a world away from the spacious Uighur houses of the oases with their wonderful courtyards. They seemed to have been built by people who were new to the idea of houses, who understood nothing about their possibilities. They were the winter quarters of the Kazaks, part-time homes for nomads. We were treading an ancient frontier between the sedentary and the pastoral, between the farmer and the nomad, between commitment and movement. Antique harvesters lumbered through the last wheatfields like lame dinosaurs while horsemen cantered through the stubble heading for the mountains.

We stopped for breakfast at a muddy town where Vronsky and Nero tried to outmanoeuvre their hangovers with bowls of noodles and black tea. Horses dozed at their hitching posts, and white awnings were guyed over the broken pavements. I looked in on one of the shops to find a row of cowpokes seated cross-legged on the counter, dangling horsewhips in their laps. At the end of the street young men in flat caps were playing pool at outdoor tables. Beyond stood a tall brick portal. I expected a mosque but found a dusty garden, an old man amongst roses and a view of the mountains.

The tarantass pulled up outside, and I climbed aboard. An hour later we crossed the Ili river at Yamatu, Wild Horse Ferry.

I spent three days in the mountains. At Tekes there were horses waiting and we rode through a long afternoon of meadows of thyme and cow parsley. The hills were smooth as bowling greens. Mushroom-coloured yurts were dotted across pastures of slow cattle. From time to time we passed small caravans of dainty-footed donkeys, piled high with sheepskins, on their way down to Ili. The day was fresh and the air tasted of autumn.

When we took to the horses, Nero and Vronsky came back to life. The horses belonged to Vronsky's father, and he galloped ahead of us now on a favourite bay, wheeling in the long grass. The two men had been away for a year and they were riding through the landscapes of childhood.

Home was the summer pastures near Baluk-Su. Yurts were scattered across the high slopes, and voices floated down to us on the thin air long before we reached them, whoops of welcome circling the hills like birds. By the time we reached the yurts, sheep were being slaughtered.

We were enthroned in a white tent on layers of carpets. At our backs were the usual piles of tin trunks, the tools of the nomad's trade, the furniture of journeys. A bewildering series of men arrived to greet the two prodigals, trailing hordes of ruddy faced children in their wake. It was a grand homecoming and I seemed to add to the sense of festivity. They had been away for a year and had returned bearing a foreigner.

After a time dinner arrived. It consisted entirely of sheep and it became clear that no part of the animal was wasted. The feet were served up as an hors-d'oeuvre, the intestines were a great success, I believe I spotted a retainer munching on the ears, and it was only with great difficulty that I managed to fend off the eyeballs. Other parts mercifully were less easy to identify.

We slept beneath the fleece. I dreamt, almost inevitably, of Fu Wen. We were riding horses atop the walls of Xi'an. Then Fu Wen was wearing a schoolgirl coat and a beret, and we were running through the gaps in hedges in the back gardens of my childhood, galloping through games of make-believe. Later a camel caravan arrived for me, and I rode away from her and the gardens past my old home into a landscape of wild olives and glaciers with an uneasy mixture of heart-break and relief. I woke quite suddenly after this, distressed. It was still the middle of the night, and the rain was murmuring on the yurt skin in soothing undertones.

In the morning I was stiff as a corpse. The previous day I had thought myself quite the horseman. Now I staggered outside into a bright morning on wooden legs. Everything ached.

But the day was too fine to miss and after a breakfast of dry bread and sour tea I set off again, riding alone into high nameless valleys. The horse seemed to share my excitement, pricking his ears and scenting the morning. He was lively, almost playful. He knew I was a novice, but he was understanding.

I followed a long grassy valley, the tinkling bells of sheep giving voices to the hillsides. A stream sparkled between thin lines of poplars and dark cattle waded in the water meadows. Cloud shadows chased each other up the rising slopes towards the high peaks, and I felt entirely, almost bewilderingly, happy. Sore from riding, I took to walking, following sheep trails, my horse snuffling at my back.

The morning was full of birds—wheatears, stonechats, and golden orioles. Blue rollers veered across the grasses and solitary hoopoes appeared on the path ahead, dusty beguiling figures, hopping impatiently from foot to foot. I followed a track through a gully of smooth grey pebbles, climbing round a vast rock outcrop that presided over this place like a ruined fortress. Beyond I emerged in further shelving pastures which sloped on their western shores to scarps of rust-coloured rock, veined with purple and white. Fragrant clouds of meadowsweet rode on the green waves of grass, and the breeze coming down from the rocks bore the scent of water. Higher still I threw myself down in a blaze of yellow flowers while my horse started on lunch. Below us I could see the bowl of our encampment, the grey smudges of fires, the lamb pens, the moving figures and the horses tethered between the yurts. High above me a kestrel trembled in the blue air. On all sides mountains shouldered past each other, climbing away towards Mongolia in the north and Tadjikstan in the south. Up here it was possible to believe that you might see both by simply turning your head.

It seemed possible to believe anything. In these mountains reason was a frail thing. It would take little effort to conjure mountain sprites dancing across the meadows with flutes, trailing notes and silks like the apsaras of Dunhuang. This was China's version of the Land of Punt or the Kingdom of Prester John, a province of mythologies. I imagined early Chinese maps, with a hazy outline of these mountains bearing the warning, or the promise, "Here Be Dragons." The Heavenly Horses that came from these regions were said to be born of dragons, and it seemed entirely credible, lying in a bed of meadowsweet, that the Chinese should believe they could ride them to Paradise. All over these mountains the ancestors of the Kazaks were buried with their horses, as the ancient Egyptians were buried with boats. No one wanted the indignity of arriving in the next world on foot.

The sound of hooves broke my reverie. I sat up and saw my horse galloping to the lower end of the meadow. He drew up suddenly, his head thrown back, then swung round and galloped a little further before stopping again. I looked uphill towards the rock escarpment. A dozen sheep were running through the yellow grass on the far edge of the meadows, blue-grey figures, their backs rolling through the long grass. The view of the mountains, the smoky domestic scene below, all suddenly seemed to fall away as my attention was focused on these running creatures, abandoning the paradise of their pasture. With their flight, the world was suddenly taut and expectant.

Then the wolves trotted into view, two silver animals and one the colour of faded gold. They moved almost leisurely across the rising ground at the base of the rocks, fanning out as they went. In this clear air, even at a distance of 500 yards I could see the ruffs on their necks, their flattened ears, their eyes fixed on the running sheep.

As the sheep gained the higher ground, the wolves quickened their pace. Panic had gripped the little flock, which veered this way and that until finally and fatally the individuals abandoned one another, and the group broke apart. With the usual precision of hunters, the wolves closed on the slowest, running now like cats. They caught it on a slope of gravel, snapping at its heels, breaking the joints and bringing it down in a flurry of fur and dust. It struggled briefly, kicking feebly at the wolves before surrendering to shock and death.

The rest of the flock, trembling on inaccessible ledges, averted their gaze.

In the evening there was a dance. I had imagined wild Kazak music, a fevered strumming of instruments, and high shouting voices. I had hoped for the Dance of the Black Stallion which involves somersaults and men standing on their heads.

Instead Glenn Miller cooed from a cassette player and sedate couples formed in the moonlight. This is what unites this country, I thought. The only links between Wang on the Bund in Shanghai and these mountain nomads two thousand miles away are the foxtrot and the ever-popular two-step. Up here in the Mountains of Heaven, they seemed as good a reason as any to have a country.

Ten

THE ENTERTAINERS

There are few destinations so delightful as one that other people have over-looked. No one came to Kuqa, not even the Chinese. It was a thoroughly Uighur town with shady lanes bordered by water channels and elaborate turquoise and pink gateways set into the long adobe walls. In the evenings the flat-capped boys played pool at outdoor tables until the muezzin called them away to prayer. On bazaar days the streets filled up with country folk and the river banks of the old town became a mêlée of carts and horses and camels and bright awnings and hard bargaining.

In the absence of guests the hotel was disintegrating. It was a collection of low buildings set round a forecourt of overripe chyrsanthemums. The gatehouse acted as reception. My room was full of frogs, refugees from the stream beyond the wall, and in the mornings one had to be careful where one trod. Once I found a frog asleep in my drinking cup. He was over-weight and apologetic.

The washing facilities consisted of a standpipe in a coal shed. However careful I was climbing back over the slag heap in the darkness, I inevitably emerged looking like a miner at the end of his shift. I took to washing late at night in the froggy stream, lowering myself into a bath of moonlight under a bower of willow branches. Such indecency had to be guarded in this Muslim town and when a donkey-cart passed on the road above, I submerged in clouds of bubbles.

The only other guests in my hotel were in the next room, a quartet of Chinese, two men and two women, who shared their accommodation with an apparently inexhaustible supply of soap powder. Each morning a donkey-cart arrived which they piled high with bright blue boxes of Chinese Daz, then set off to market. In Kuqa the demand for soap powder seemed insatiable and every evening they returned with the donkey-cart empty. I bought a couple of boxes myself at a knock-down price. It shifted coal grime wonderfully.

The quartet were a secretive lot, deflecting social overtures and keeping to themselves. Their manner and their habit of storing soap powder in remote hotel rooms suggested criminality. I saw them as the frontmen in an elaborate soap powder conspiracy. Their furtive lifestyle sat heavily with them. In the evenings the men got drunk in their room among the boxes of Daz while the women strolled hand-in-hand in the dust road outside the gate, their heads tilted together.

The Daz Gang must have been unsettled by Kuqa's way with criminals. On bazaar days convicts toured the town as the centrepiece of merry cavalcades of police and army vehicles. The parade was led by an army truck from which a camera crew filmed the whole proceedings. Next came twenty police motor-cycles with lights flashing. In the side-cars sat the shaven-headed prisoners, handcuffed to the petrol tanks, sullen fellows ill-disposed to joining in the fun. Behind them the mood lightened with endless jeeps of fat policemen picking their teeth and waving at the crowds. Behind these came truck-loads of soldiers with hard hats and fixed bayonets. Despite their state of battle readiness they shared the carnival mood, laughing and waving like celebrities. Traveling at speed with sirens wailing, the cavalcade toured the town relentlessly, like politicians at election time. They broke for lunch at midday, then started up again in the afternoon. Later the hotel manager told me that the soldiers had shot the prisoners at sunset.

One afternoon a Japanese man turned up at my hotel, dressed entirely in white and dragging a heavy suitcase behind him. He was given the other bed in my room and popped his head round the door like a spring-up toy. He was delighted to hear I lived in England. I was, he announced, his first English person.

Though Shusaku was rather large for a Japanese, he had a weightless manner, a lightness of being. He floated about the room like a great white moth, his hands delicately cocked at the wrist. He was an innocent abroad with a wide trusting face behind rimless spectacles. In spite of the coal shed he was always immaculate in white. Every morning he dined on a banquet of vitamin pills and dietary supplements. Every evening he washed his clothes. Once I woke in the middle of the night to find him washing socks by torchlight. It was his good fortune to have a supply of inexpensive soap powder so close to hand.

His English was eccentric, and conversation was made laborious by his habit of repeating everything I said very slowly, as if looking for hidden nuances. Left to his own devices, he chatted continually to himself, exchanges which were punctuated with little exclamations of surprise and delight. His world was full of the unexpected, and whatever he did was accompanied by these startled notes of surprise. The only book he had with him was the Bible. He was an avid fan of the Old Testament, particularly the Book of Genesis. But he was a Buddhist. His journey to China was a pilgrimage, retracing the long journey of Buddhism across China to Japan.

We shared a hired car to visit the Kizil caves which lie fifty miles to the west where the Muzart river bends through empty hills. They are the oldest Buddhist shrines in China, dating back to the third century. Though they are less extensive and less famous than the shrines at Dunhuang, many scholars believe them to contain some of the finest Buddhist art in Central Asia.

I was familiar now with these journeys to the past, to silent kingdoms marooned in the dessert, picturesque with visions of Paradise. One crossed a sudden frontier from green lanes into a glaring wilderness of stones. The last trees of Kuqa staggered in drifts of sand, and the desert was overtaken by graves, marked by sticks and rags, the banners of permanent exile. Shusaku pressed his face to the window and uttered a long sigh of surprise and awe.

Far out in the desert we passed a ruined watch-tower overlooking a river of slate-coloured pebbles. Straddling the dry flood bed were the bare ribs of the city of Subash, great in the fourth century. The ruins were sliding into the dessert round the feet of a giant stupa. Inside the temple, among the lizards and the skeletons of birds, I found Shusaku chanting.

Further still the road skirted convoluted rock formations, like gangs of petrified giants. Then it veered away through Salt Water Gully, a red gorge with saline stains around the lips of a depleted river, to emerge into yet wider desert flanked by wind-scarred hills the colour of camels. At midday we fell from the hills into a panorama of water, a river framed by purple mountains. Along the banks were glades of mulberry and poplar trees.

In a lane we met a policeman who demanded to see our passports, as if we were arriving in a new country. His duty done, he vanished into a building to reappear in another guise—caretaker and guide. The dark glasses had been abandoned. The policeman's jacket was replaced by a cardigan and the holster by a cluster of antique keys. Happier in his new role, he chatted about roses and nirvana as he led us up stony paths to the caves. When he opened the iron gates and the wooden doors sunlight stole across the frescos.

In the Lankavatara sutra one finds: "Everything comes from the mind, like objects appearing from the sleeve of a magician." These Buddhist caves were a conjured world produced from the sleeves of monks, as surprising and satisfying as doves. Desecration had made the frescos incomplete: in one cave a confusion of bare limbs and round bellies wandered without heads; in another a line of faces had misplaced their bodies. When one considers all the people who have vandalized these caves, it is surprising there is anything left. Local farmers hacked off the paint for fertilizer. European archaeologists cut whole frescos from the walls for their museums. Thieves carted away more for the black market. Muslim fanatics attacked the images in a religious fury, then the Red Guards followed with the same impulse.

Shusaku was overcome. He flitted among the paintings, swooning with astonishment. But in spite of his enthusiasm, none of the images detained him long. He was a junkie of first impressions, addicted to that initial moment of surprise. Occasionally he broke away from their spell long enough to cry, "This one. Look, look." But before I could respond he was off again. By the end he was quite demented, running round the tombs, his face a few inches from the frescos, giggling uncontrollably.

The world that produced these caves was hardly a provincial backwater. When Xuan Zang paused here on his way to India, Kuqa was the capital of an irrigated kingdom the size of England, with its own language and distinct cultural traditions. Two huge Buddhas, reminiscent of the Colossi of Memnon, stood outside its western gates. Xuan wrote that its "air was soft, and its inhabitants elegantly dressed in ornamental silks." Despite its numerous monasteries and powerful priesthood Kuqa was a worldly place, a decadent and lavish feudal society. "Virtues are not treasured but wealth is worshipped," commented Xuan disapprovingly.

In the Buddhist art of Central Asia Kizil represents a more western school, with few of the Chinese influences so evident at Turfan and especially at Dunhuang. Here the influences are almost entirely Indian and Iranian, the latter bearing a strong Hellenistic imprint. The decorative motifs and the fashions of the figures were those of the Sassanian court in fourth-century Persia. The prominent citizens of Kuqa, who paid for much of the work at Kizil, still stalk the walls, proprietorial among the visions of Paradise. With their oiled hair and thin curling moustaches and layered gowns, these knights and their handsome wives were strangely familiar.

The Sassanian era was one of Asia's *belles époques,* a glamorous age dominated by a new breed of nobleman, mannered, refined, and chivalrous. Its influence was widespread and, through the medium of the Arabs and the Crusades, Sassanian ideals had informed the rising aspirations of the medieval feudal lord in a Europe emerging from the Dark Ages. This was where I had seen the great and the good of Kuqa before. Joined by a common influence, they had the same stylish confidence as Norman knights. The patrons of the Kizil caves were the cousins of the stone effigies in English parish churches half a world away.

In the evening I took Shusaku to a concert. The caves had been almost too much for him and I thought he needed to unwind. In the car he had chattered obsessively about *karma* before falling into a troubled sleep punctuated by bouts of chanting.

The idea of concerts seemed new to Shusaku, and he prepared for the evening as for an expedition, kitting himself out with a Swiss army knife, a change of shirt and a canteen of sterilized water. The concert was held in an open-air cinema. The audience, young Uighurs in flat caps, sat on rows of low benches eating nuts and spitting the shells into each other's laps.

The first singer was a man in a dinner-jacket, a big man with a big voice. The audience ignored him. They were otherwise engaged, chatting, buying more nuts, hailing their friends, and playing cards. The sound of gunfire came over a low wall from the television set in a café next door, and a long row of figures stood on benches at the side to watch the western.

Attention reverted momentarily for the next act—a remarkable young woman in a shimmering gold ball gown. Closely fitted at the hem, the gown made her look like a mermaid. It also made her flap back and forth across the stage like a mermaid, which was a pity, for she sang beautifully.

These two were merely warm-up acts. The star turn, the woman that everyone had come to see, was Miriam Nazir. She was introduced hysterically by the man in the dinner-jacket. A spotlight swept the stage then passed over the audience. We turned in our seats to see a door opening in an old bus parked at the back of the cinema. Into the beam of light stepped a buxom woman in a spangly dress smiling like Mae West. "Oh," whispered Shusaku. "Such teeth."

Her grand entrance was not a success. As Miriam made her way down the aisle towards the stage, waving at her people, an obstruction—a nut seller in argument with his customers—forced her to cut along one of the rows. Many of the occupants were slow to move and Miriam, brilliantly spotlit, looked like a mad woman waving her arms at the end of a slow queue.

But she was nothing if not a trooper, and once she had escaped Row G, she took the stage by storm. After a few numbers she made several forays back into the audience, patrolling the aisles like a music hall *artiste* working the punters. I saw an ageing bloated face as she passed, garish with make-up. She greeted me surprisingly in English. "How do you do," she said in a cracked voice, shaking my hand.

The evening broke up after her act, the audience rising as one and crowding towards the doors as if suddenly remembering it had better things to do. Swept along on this tide Shusaku and I washed up against the chest of a huge man by the exit. He handed us a note. It was written in red ink on flimsy rice paper, folded twice: "It was nice to meet you. Please come to take tea with me. Wishes, Miriam."

The burly retainer motioned us towards the bus, thumped on the rear door twice, then jerked it open without waiting for a response. Nudging us inside, he slammed the door behind us.

We found ourselves in a small space curtained off from the rest of the bus. There were chairs and a table with a mirror, a full ashtray, and crumpled tissue paper bloodied with lipstick. In a corner was a bucket where empty soft drink bottles floated among cigarette butts. Shusaku unscrewed his canteen and gulped water.

Presently Miriam emerged from behind the curtain knotting a regal-looking dressing-gown. The gregarious performer had been replaced by a haughty disdainful figure. She offered her hand rather icily, motioned for us to sit, then swept the soiled tissues off the table into the water bucket.

"Are you smoking?" she asked. "Marlyboros, Johnny Players, Benson and Heavens?"

We said we weren't. She sighed and took a packet of cheap Chinese cigarettes from her dressing-gown pocket. We sat like schoolboys in detention. Shusaku had folded his hands in his lap.

"Chai," Miriam screamed suddenly. She got up and kicked the door three times. "Tea, tea, tea."

She sat down again, lighting her cigarette and bestowing a faint smile upon us. Once she must have been beautiful. Now the face was collapsing, abandoning the fine bones that had helped to make her name. The cheeks were muddy with rouge and the eyes, behind grilles of mascara, were stony. She exuded exhaustion. Her fingers were short and splayed, adorned with heavy rings and nicotine stains.

"I enjoyed the show," I said, feeling I needed to cheer her up. Shusaku nodded feverishly.

She waved her hand dismissively. "These audiences," she sighed. "Monkeys. Have you been to Urumqi? In Urumqi people can appreciate." The last word was like a curse. "I tour of course. Abroad, I mean. Alma Ata, Tashkent, Samarkand." The names conjured an allure almost as faded as her own. She leaned forward, and a gold necklace, lounging on the broad fields of her bosom, plunged indecently into her cleavage.

At this moment hysterical laughter broke out beyond the curtain. A man and a woman, shrieking between gasps of breath, seemed to be tickling one another. The bus shook.

"I am surrounded by children," Miriam said, throwing up her hands. "Who can I talk to?"

The laughter stopped suddenly and the curtains opened. It was the mermaid and the big man. He still wore his dinner-jacket but she had changed into a blue track suit. Two long pigtails fell over her shoulders. Sultry sophistication had given way to a girlish timidity. The big man shook my hand while the mermaid giggled, clutching the curtain like someone discovered in the shower. Miriam glowered at them, as though they were gatecrashers. Then the door flew open and the retainer hoisted himself into the bus with a tea-tray and a grunt.

We were now six where two would have been a crowd.

With the tea the retainer dealt cigarettes like playing cards. We tried to decline but he would not countenance such rudeness. He stuck cigarettes in our mouths and lit them. Shusaku spluttered. The mermaid has disengaged from her curtain and was slurping tea through piscine lips.

"But you have not been introduced," Miriam cried. She supplied the names of the two singers. "I took them on some years ago in Urumqi. After the Cultural Revolution it was difficult to find good singers. He was a cleaner at the theatre. I felt sorry for him."

The big man stood up, toppling his chair. "They made me be a cleaner." His face had gone dark. "I was a dancer. I trained at the Institute. The Chinese forced me to be a cleaner."

"Control yourself, please." Miriam waved her cigarette at him. "Remember our guests."

The cleaner-cum-dancer was unsure how to retake his seat with dignity until the retainer, who looked like the Xinjiang heavyweight champion, bellowed: "Sit down."

The mermaid let out a little squeak of merriment, then tried to cover it up as if she had broken wind.

Miriam turned her gaze towards her.

"Is it so funny?" she asked. "Where would you be today? Working as a room attendant in some hotel?"

At this the mermaid burst into tears with bewildering suddenness and fled beyond the curtain. The cleaner-dancer ran after her, Miriam shouted abuse in their wake and the retainer dealt another hand of cigarettes. Soon afterwards we made our excuses and left. Miriam took our departure as a slight and refused to say goodbye.

Shusaku was terribly distressed by the evening, and spent all night sighing and muttering about the entertainers. In the morning he wrote out some Buddhist sutras on a piece of white card and took it round to the cinema. But the bus was gone. They had left for Khotan. There were still three weeks of the tour to run.

In the last fields of Kuqa, sand dunes rode through the crops like humpbacked whales. Dawn glazed the empty road, and the desert cold crept into the bus through ill-fitting windows. To the north lay a low line of rumpled hills. From the south green and black marshes closed on the road, presenting us briefly with visions of moorhens pushing through tall reeds. Later the marshes retreated and disappeared like another mirage, leaving a vast sweep of ash-coloured emptiness.

It was a jolly bus. Hand luggage consisted of boxes of apples and everyone wore hats. The front rows were occupied by a flying squadron of the Chinese air force, ten pilots in crumpled blue uniforms and a collection of ill-fitting caps. They breakfasted on dry bread, played a few hands of rummy, then opened charts to study our course. No one seemed to be in the least concerned that the air force was travelling by public bus.

My neighbour was a dour fellow in a lambswool hat. On his lap he cradled a black doctor's bag which held scraps of old newspaper for rolling his cigarettes. The splendidly dextrous way he rolled them was rather spoiled by the fact that they gradually fell apart as he smoked them, showering our laps with burning newsprint. He was a singer, and gazed morosely out the window singing a series of laments as flat and monotonous as the landscape. Each dirge came with an almost inexhaustible supply of verses.

At Aksu he was replaced by another dour fellow in a lambswool hat. He was so similar to his predecessor that they might have been brothers who patronized the same milliner. The second man found me astonishing, and couldn't take his eyes off me. He touched my hair, fingered my trousers, and insisted I remove my shoes that he might examine them. When I took out a book to read he lifted it silently from my hands, and peered incomprehendingly at it for long minutes. But I got used to him; his great virtue was that he did not sing. Eventually he fell asleep in my lap.

Across the aisle was a fat man in a thin man's suit. In his confined seat he bulged impressively, and I feared for the seams of his jacket. Even his hat looked as if it might fly off at any moment under pressure.

Conversation turned to currencies and I produced a ten-pound note which received a gratifyingly awed reception. In his capacity as a man of the world—he had been to Pakistan once—the fat man took charge, explaining its implications to the other passengers. He identified the Queen as the great British Padshah, Lilibut the Second. When he turned it over, and found another woman on the reverse, he identified her as the former Padshah, Queen Lilibut the First. I explained that she was in fact Florence Nightingale, a famous nurse. The news sent the currency into immediate free-fall. The passengers gazed at my tenner as if it was Albanian *lehs*. In China nurses are citizens of lowly reputation.

The most striking figure on the bus was a splendid fellow who sat opposite the air force amid a bevy of women. He wore a tall velvet hat with fox-fur trim which bumped the ceiling of the bus. Thick eyebrows were pitched like awnings over bright deep-set eyes and a Roman nose. When he smiled, gold teeth twinkled. He had tall boots and an overcoat with a floral lining.

He came to sit across the aisle from me with a series of dietary questions. He was greatly relieved to hear that I didn't eat donkeys or dogs, but was disappointed about the pigs. The Chinese, he said, making a face, eat everything that moves.

He was concerned about my lack of a *khanum,* a wife. A man must have a wife, he declared. The whole bus, captivated by the novelty of a foreigner speaking even rudimentary Uighur, craned over the backs of their seat. They all agreed. A man must have a wife, they chorused.

My friend was shocked that I had got this far without one.

"You must start looking immediately," he cried. "Time is of the essence."

He leaned across the aisle. "I will tell you what to look for. I know. I have four wives."

"First," he went on, "a small mouth and large eyes. Second, a wife must not be too tall, or too short. Third, the nose. If it is too big it might present difficulties for kissing."

"Finally," my friend declared, "you must not overlook the breasts."

He glared at me for confirmation. I assured him I had absolutely no intention of overlooking the breasts.

"Good," he said. "The breasts are very important. It is essential that they be buoyant. Buoyant breasts are the thing." The other passengers nodded in unison.

Later he returned to the company of women at the front of the bus. His wives were aloof creatures with their arms round each other's shoulders. Nestling among them the patriarch became a boy. They took his hat off and straightened his jacket. They sent him to fetch apples from the luggage rack. They shushed him when he grew boisterous, and put him to sleep in the corner.

At a police road-block near Artush, a problem arose about the driver's papers. He didn't have any. I had wondered for some time whether he was a driver at all. He drove at moderate speed, showed unusual courtesy to other vehicles, and rarely used his horn. It was all highly suspicious.

The police arrested him, chaining him to a bench behind their guard hut. Keen to get to Kashgar, the passengers assembled a delegation of the most diplomatic of their number to lobby for his release. I was included in the hope that the disruption of a foreigner's journey might sway our appeal if all else failed. It worked. The driver was allowed to complete the drive to Kashgar, about an hour away. We proceeded like a presidential convoy with police vehicles fore and aft, their lights flashing.

In the wide oasis of Kashgaria the ponds and water channels were golden in the twilight. By the time we reached the town it was dark, and we nosed our way through unlit streets. At a dusty corner the driver stopped suddenly, leapt down from the bus and fled into side alleys pursued by the police. We got out and began to unrope our bags from the roof.

I took a donkey-cart to the hotel. In the narrow lanes of the bazaar bearded merchants in gas-lit shops sat amongst their wares. We threaded through dense crowds of veiled women and turbanned men, parted by riders astride dainty-footed donkeys. Clouds of smoke from the evening cooking stalls enveloped the whole scene. Finally we rattled down a long avenue of old trees past the remnants of the city walls and turned through a large gateway. On the pillar I glimpsed the name: the Hotel Semen.

Eleven

ON SECRET SERVICE

"Before the coming of the telegraph and the aeroplane," wrote Peter Hop-kirk, "the small mud-walled township of Kashgar was one of the loneliest and most inaccessible places on earth." It had long been so. When the geographer Ptolemy included Kashgar in his map of the world in the second century AD, he placed it in the same neighbourhood as Horse-Eating Scyths, Cannibals, and Terra Incognita, as if it might be only a city of rumour. Yet in these regions Kashgar seemed a metropolis. To the traveller in Central Asia, Peter Fleming commented in 1936, "its outlandish name spelt Civilization."

Kashgar was one of the stages for the Great Game, that Victorian Cold War played out in Central Asia between the British and the Russian empires. In an age when Chinese Turkestan was as remote as Antarctica, both powers began to perceive it as a vital sphere of influence, particularly in the light of Beijing's frail grip on the area. The Russians, who had already absorbed much of western Turkestan from the Caspian Sea to Alma Ata, established a Consulate at Kashgar in 1882, staffed by the formidable Count Nikolai Petrovsky, "a militant Anglophobe." The British, anxious about any threat to the northern passes into British India, sent their own agent eight years later.

In this lonely place the two consulates were the centre of a tiny European community which included a couple of Swedish missionaries, fun-seeking Calvinists, and a Dutch priest with whom Macartney, the British agent, conversed in Latin. To visiting explorers, archaeologists, missionaries and spies, trooping across the wastes of Xinjiang, the consulates offered an oasis of civilization: baths and fresh linen, iced drinks, armchairs and illustrated periodicals, all served up in the atmosphere of a country house.

But beneath the social niceties, Kashgar was bubbling with all the intrigues of international espionage. The two consuls were there to keep an eye on one another, and there was a marvellous hypocrisy in their relations. Between dinner parties, they were steaming open each other's mail. Between tennis tournaments and garden fêtes, they were trying to have each other thrown out of the country. House guests were presumed to be spies, servants were double agents, and banquets, enlivened with Russian vodka, were peppered with assassinations.

The two old consulates, which stand within a half mile of each other, are now the town's chief hotels. In this transformation Chini Bagh, the British Consulate, has fared rather badly. A shoddy multi-storeyed block has been built in its front garden, housing Pakistani traders and dysenteric backpackers, while the old house has been reduced to "The Flavorsome Restaurant."

The Russian Consulate has been more fortunate. Gloomy lines of birch and cypress trees still line the drive past the peeling dachas. In the reception rooms the tall windows are shuttered against the light and the dust, and the red velvet curtains hanging over the doors give entrances and exits a sense of theatre. A high garden wall beyond thickets of old roses and a collapsing conservatory still keep the native town at bay. But chief among the pleasures of the Hotel Semen is Colonel Petrovsky's bath, an antique construction of Russian proportions. After the coal shed in Kuqa, it was the greatest luxury Kashgar could offer.

On a dreary boulevard not far from the bus station is a monolithic statue of Mao, one of the last in China, raising a hand of comradeship to urchins kicking deflated footballs in the stony expanse of People's Park. In these revisionary times attempts have been made to remove the Great Helmsman, but he has been constructed in such a way, shrewd politician that he was, that his demolition would threaten neighbouring buildings. So he remains, presiding over the city he tried to destroy.

Liberation was a tragedy for Kashgar. A distant and preoccupied Chinese administration was suddenly replaced by an energetic regime whose idea of government went beyond the occasional telegram. Young Chinese cadres arrived, intent on creating a brave new world in their own image. They tore down the old city walls and began to plough their dreaded boulevards through Kashgar's warren of old lanes. Their talk of comradeship tended to blur the distinctions between Chinese and Turkic peoples, so important to the Uighar sense of identity. Marxism made employees of people accustomed to an economy that revolved around the bazaar. The Cultural Revolution became an attack on Turkic culture, focused on the mosque. The Uighur language was forced to abandon its traditional Arabic script, Islam was denounced, the Koran banned, mullahs arrested or sent to the countryside, and the great Id Kah mosque ransacked by Red Guards.

Kashgar survived, in the same way it survived Genghis Khan, by keeping its head down and waiting for the storm to pass. In these more relaxed times, the mosque has reasserted its place in Uighur life and the bazaar, now free of all restriction, is once again the centre of economic life. But the increased freedom has only allowed anti-Chinese sentiment a voice. Massive programmes of Chinese settlement may have made the Turkic peoples a minority in their own land, but here in Kashgar the Chinese are still only 10 percent of the population. Most of these are government officials and soldiers presiding over a people that have grown increasingly restless under Chinese rule.

In the dusty sunlit lanes of Kashgar, all the races of Central Asia paraded in their hats: Uzbeks with flat faces and narrow trilbys, Kazaks ruddy from the mountains beneath utilitarian flat caps, hawk-faced Tadjiks in frock coats and turbans, Uighurs in long cotton shirts and pretty embroidered pillboxes, Kirghiz booted like storm troopers beneath sheepskin bonnets. In these crowds the Han Chinese stood out, not so much for their drabness or their lack of swagger, as for the lack of a good hat. Hats are to Central Asia what the motor car is to North Americans: it is impossible to go outside without one.

In the workshops of Kashgar, millinery is rivalled only by trunk-making. Whole streets are given over to trunk makers, feverishly hammering patterns into the gold-colored tin that gaudily decorates the chests spilling out of their narrow shops into the roadway. It is a good life whose essentials are a trunk and a decent hat.

In neighbouring streets boot-makers blackened with polish were hammering heels on tall riding boots. Round the corner a farrier was shoeing horses, each one trussed and immobilized with an elaborate rigging of ropes. Cartwrights were stacking huge spoked wheels and carpenters, knee deep in shavings, were building beds. In a lane where children chased hoops saddlers were polishing the plumed harnesses of horses.

In shallow booths along the market streets the jewellers and curio sellers reclined on cushions amongst antique hand mirrors, pre-revolutionary roubles, snuff-boxes and ear-rings like horse ornaments. In the alley of cloth sellers, where the stalls were separated by sheets of bright colour, there was an unusual hush, a stillness amid the silks and vivid rolls of cotton. The merchants dozed on their wares while gangs of hooded women conferred in whispers.

In the market streets the crowds thickened between gaily balconied houses. The tarantass drivers beneath their red awnings cracked long whips, the donkey cart drivers cleared paths with shouts of *"boish, boish,"* and the cyclists with chickens dangling from their handlebars wobbled and rang their bells. A man in a felt cloak and a pirate's moustache loped by on a long-legged camel while another herded fat-tailed sheep through the legs of ironmongers hawking nails by the bucketful. Fruit sellers moulded tall pyramids of purple figs, dried apricots and raisins, sugar salesmen set about huge sugar loaves with hatchets, arms dealers laid out dazzling displays of decorated knives while outside the noodle shops the cooks, rolling out long sausages of pastry, stretched and divided them into noodles like magicians performing rope tricks.

In front of Id Kah, the largest mosque in China, madmen and philosophers waggled their straggling beards while under the clock tower the pigeon fanciers gathered for an impromptu market, pulling prize birds from the depths of their trousers. The best white doves were going for a pound.

In the square a crowd had gathered to watch a bare-chested fellow in a cocked hat and a red sash. He was a cross between a song-and-dance man and the local doctor. While his two sons did cartwheels he offered the rows of hatted and veiled figures a miracle cure in the form of sticky bits of paper, heated and applied to stiff shoulders, bad backs, aching knees, warts and speech impediments. For the climax of the show the Entertainer broke bricks on his sons' stomachs, apparently crippling them for life. But after a brief course of the sticky paper they were right as rain. The crowd clamoured for the right to buy.

At sunset the muezzin called and files of men trooped through the mosque portal into a vast courtyard, said to hold eight thousand worshippers. Among the lime trees and the rush-matted porticos they assembled in obedient ranks, murmuring submission, kneeling and prostrating in unison towards Mecca. As they filed out women waited by the gates holding up loaves of bread. The faithful spat on the loaves, which were then carried home for the sick.

After prayers the men waded through clouds of charcoal smoke to the food stalls and dinners of grilled mutton, warm nan and tea. With darkness the stall owners lit huge hurricane lamps and the men settled down to second helpings and the gossip of the bazaar. Dinner, like prayer, was an entirely masculine world.

Something of Kashgar's cloak-and-dagger atmosphere, that balance of melodrama and farce, still clung to the old town. The place was thick with secret organizations, plots, spies and informers. I was only three days in Kashgar before I was enlisted as a foreign agent.

I was buying stamps in the post office when a young man with a flat cap and a struggling moustache sidled up to me under the pretext of examining a notice-board.

"Meet me in the tea-house behind the Id Kah," he whispered before sidling away again.

I don't usually accept assignations from strange men in post offices, but I had an idea who he was. I had already discussed politics with a receptionist at my hotel who had said he would put me in touch with someone who could answer more of my questions. His furtive manner had led me to expect an equally furtive approach.

I found my contact on the tea-house balcony overlooking a street of hat shops and pack camels. Anvar was that most dangerous of figures: a revolutionary living in someone else's courtyard. He was a Uighur nationalist plotting the overthrow of Chinese rule in Xinjiang and the establishment of an independent East Turkestan. He asked me if I had seen the sign on the roundabout near my hotel.

"It is in Chinese. It exhorts settlers 'to build their second homeland'," he said. "What people have the right to a second homeland? This is Turkestan. It is our homeland, not a second homeland for the Chinese." He spoke to me in English so that our neighbours on the balcony could not understand.

The tea came and Anvar took crumpled sheets of paper from the lining of his jacket. I was bracing myself for political treatises when he began to read me poems. Between the poems he told me tales of past revolts and planned insurrections. The two began to flow together, the poems and the revolution, so that the verses, about love and loss, seemed to become calls to arms while the stories of guerrilla warfare were dreamy and rather lyrical. It was a familiar vice, this confusion of politics with private griefs and passions.

It was difficult to know how much poetic licence infiltrated his accounts of recent unrest in Xinjiang. Much of what he told me I was later able to confirm from other sources, but the details were occasionally questionable, as if these stories were already part of the mythology on which nations are built. His themes were betrayal and vengeance and heroism. They had a Biblical quality. Even horses played their part.

Early in 1990 secessionist forces had planned an uprising that was to begin in the village of Aktu about thirty miles south of Kashgar. Like other Uighurs who talked to me about events at Aktu, he whispered its name as if the word had become a treasonable offence.

Over a period of months, arms and munitions had been collected, many of them acquired locally, others smuggled across the border from Pakistan. Cells of rebels began training, and secret lines of communication were established. Aktu was naturally fortified, and at a signal men from all over Kashgaria would gather there to take over the town in an uprising that was meant to spread via other cells to the whole of Xinjiang.

The plot had gone wrong in the bazaar in Kashgar. One of the rebels had been sent to the city to buy a horse, and had set his heart on a beautiful grey mare, a tall creature of a breed now rare in China, related to the great Turcoman horses of Ferghana. But the bargaining had not gone well, and he could not beat the horse-dealer down to his best offer. In the heat of argument, the Uighur had pleaded with him, saying his people needed this horse, that he must allow him to have it for the sake of Turkestan. His remark was overhead. The Chinese secret police operate an extensive network of informers.

A series of arrests followed, and under torture the planned uprising was discovered. When word reached the secessionist leadership already assembled in Aktu, they decided to move immediately before the Chinese had the opportunity to swoop. They stormed the army post and the Public Security Bureau, killing the Chinese officials. But the expected uprisings throughout the rest of Xinjiang never materialized. The Chinese, forewarned, had stepped up their usual security measures and rounded up the usual suspects. The men in Aktu were isolated. Tanks and planes were brought in and the town subjected to intensive bombardment, killing men, women, and children. The uprising was over almost before it began. Riots broke out in Kashgar and other towns of Xinjiang but they were quickly and ruthlessly quelled. The unrest in 1990 was, however, sufficient for the Chinese to close the Kashgar area to foreigners and to seal the border with Pakistan. It was not reopened until 1992.

As Anvar was ending this story a man sat down at a neighbouring table. He was dressed like a pantomime spy in an amateur production. He wore a trilby and dark glasses. He had turned up the collar of his suit. He smoked without taking the cigarette out of his mouth. He looked like George Raft on a bad day.

As he drank tea and ate cigarettes he kept shuffling his chair, gradually moving closer and closer to our table. Anvar had begun to talk of innocuous matters, the weather, his family. George Raft was now virtually in my lap.

When we got up to go, the pantomime spy followed. In the street Anvar walked quickly, dodging through the crowds. Rounding a corner we slipped into an eating-house, full of long tables and steam, and crossed straight through to the kitchen. The cooks, presumably familiar with Anvar's entrances and exits, hardly looked up as we opened a back door and stepped into an alley of blacksmiths.

I was having a wonderful time, playing cops and robbers with George Raft in a remote location in Central Asia. I even got to do the old back door of the restaurant ploy.

But Anvar was not amused. He was shaking.

"Who was he?" I asked.

"Secret police," he said.

"He wasn't very secret."

"They don't like people talking to foreigners."

He was anxious, glancing continually over his shoulder. His hands were trembling. "I must go. Come to see me tomorrow," he said. "I need your help. I will leave instructions at your hotel."

That evening the receptionist handed me a little hand-drawn map. It was directions to Anvar's house.

The next morning I found the place in one of the older districts where the houses had grown over the winding lanes, making them tunnels. Donkey-carts wheeled unexpectedly round corners and children skipped between dusty shafts of sunlight. Through doors left ajar I glimpsed courtyards enclosed by vines and long verandas of carpets. Women gazed out at me as I passed.

Anvar lived in a courtyard. The house was deserted and locked. The owner, he said, allowed him to stay in the courtyard because he was a member of the Organization. His bed roll lay on the veranda, a small cat asleep at its foot. There was a primus stove and a tall wooden desk covered with his sheets of paper. Anvar was packing, plucking his clothes from the painted railings where they were drying.

"I must leave," he said. "A message has come from Urumqi."

He threw his clothes into a satchel, and ferried his few belongings, a bowl, a kettle, a lantern, to a hideaway on the roof. I wondered if his hasty departure had anything to do with George Raft.

At the desk he shuffled papers. "Will you post some letters for me?"

"Sure," I said.

"In Pakistan. It is not safe for me to post them here in China. They are watching me." He was folding the letters and putting them into envelopes. "Will you write the addresses?" I copied the destinations onto the envelopes. They were to contacts abroad, in America, in Pakistan, and in Saudi Arabia. One was to the military attaché of a foreign embassy in Beijing. "They are secret letters. About our Organization. They will not search your luggage because you are a foreigner. Anyway they will think they are your letters and will not bother with them."

I put them in my pocket. "I must hurry now," he said. "Thank you. We are grateful for your help."

He looked out through the keyhole of the door to see that the alley was empty then shook my hand and let me out, locking the door behind me.

Over 100,000 people are said to attend the Sunday bazaar in Kashgar. From long before dawn, the roads into the town were clogged with traffic. Horse- and donkey-carts were nose to tail. Young men in a hurry, standing with their whips, were overtaking like charioteers. Horsemen and camel riders avoided the crush by cutting through the fields. Everyone arrived *en famille*, unmarried daughters and shrunken grannies riding on top of the donkey fodder, among the chickens and the sacks of produce. For years the bazaar was banned, but now under a more relaxed economic regime this orgy of buying and selling has regained its old place as the high-point of Kashgar's social calendar, the place to see and be seen.

You can get anything in the Kashgar bazaar—a new chimney, a fox-fur hat, seed corn, a wardrobe, some sheep, a spittoon, an overcoat, roof rafters, horseshoes, a horse, a cradle, a camel. By mid morning the crowds are almost impenetrable, the cart parks are a Chinese puzzle of upturned yokes and the massed donkeys tethered beneath shade trees are already biting each other's rumps in donkey feuds.

As in any eastern bazaar the trades stick together, the better to control the market. Lines of bearded apothecaries surrounded by little sacks of strange powders and roots awaited the sick with dour faces and mortars and pestles. Tailors giving al fresco fittings of marvellous waistcoats melted into lines of barbers busy shaving the scalps of bearded patriarchs who then hurried off to Hat Alley. Round the corner in the underwear department women in veils and orthopaedic stockings were bargaining for pink negligées with daring necklines. Between the horseshoe sellers and the inner tube salesmen were the paint sellers, their white beards stained with pigment, spooning little piles of powdered colour onto squares of newspaper.

The most exciting section of the bazaar was the horse market. At its heart was a bare stretch of earth where prospective buyers, keen to test-drive the goods, galloped up and down in clouds of dust, swerving their mounts this way and that to check their responsiveness. A stubbornly unresponsive mule upset three melon carts and galloped through the crowd bearing an elderly gentlemen. Neither was seen again.

Many of the riders were daredevil boys, hired by the owners to show off their wares. They spun and wheeled their mounts like skateboarders. Greybeards, acting as roving inspectors, drifted through the crowds ready to give their opinion of a horse to uncertain buyers by examining its teeth and feeling its skull. The bargaining was fierce, accompanied by the full range of bazaar theatrics, tempers and huffs, sudden exits and reluctant returns. Intermediaries paid five per cent by buyer and seller shuttled anxiously between the two, cajoling, bullying, searching for common ground. To keep others in ignorance of the terms the men held hands and communicated their offers and counter-offers by means of finger pressure. When a deal was struck buyer and seller pressed their palms to the earth as a symbol of their fidelity.

In this scrum of riders and animals I met my friend from the Kuqa bus, the elderly patriarch who had advised me about wives. He wore a purple dressing-gown belted with a pink sash and a knife whose handle was engraved with serpents. He shook my hand fiercely, delighted to see me, as if the bus was some trauma that bound us. His horse, he explained, had died recently and he was looking for a replacement.

"A man without a horse is only half a man," he said.

I asked him about the different breeds.

"Mainly two," he said. "The Ili horse and the Barkol." He pointed to a grey galloping up the track with an eight year old jockey. It wheeled in front of us, its mouth foaming. "It is an Ili. They are reliable, good natured. They are big horses but they do not run smoothly. The ground in Ili is stony. Most of the others are Barkol or Yanqi horses. They run more smoothly because Barkol is sandy country. They are difficult, contrary, but they never tire. The Chinese say the holes in their hearts are crooked. But what do the Chinese know? They are afraid of horses."

My friend was keen on a lovely bay, an Ili, a big lean horse with a powerful turn of speed and a noble bearing. He mounted it and rode up and down the track. He was a fine seat, a dignified old man, erect and serious, manipulating the horse with the slightest turn of the reins. Horse and rider looked made for each other. I could see the old man had his heart set on it. An adolescent passion was creeping into his expression. He conferred with the intermediary from the saddle as if he could not bring himself to dismount in case the horse and the deal escaped him. I feared his eagerness was too transparent for a good price, and left him to his bargaining.

The most sought-after goods in the bazaar were among the most worthless. Pakistani traders were selling cheap costume jewellery and the fever among the local women for these baubles was incredible. They fought to get their hands on them, almost tearing the traders limb from limb. It was common to see Pakistanis pursued through the bazaar by gangs of veiled women. I found one hiding in the timber yard.

"Business is good," I said.

He shrugged. "What is common in one place, becomes a great rarity somewhere else." Marco Polo couldn't have put it better. It might have been the motto of the Silk Road.

Towards the end of the day I met my friend at a dumpling stall. Bulls were careering past scattering the crowds. The old man was carrying a gaily painted cradle.

"You did not buy the horse?" I asked.

"No," he said, putting on a brave face. "I bought this cradle instead. My daughter is pregnant."

I marvelled at his priorities.

"Perhaps I am too old for another horse," he said. "When a man dies it is better to leave a cradle than a horse. Besides," he winked at me, "the cradle is cheaper."

The day was over. The stalls were being dismantled, and the wagons piled with goods. On all the roads out of Kashgar donkey-carts were galloping away into the dusk.

Twelve

YAKS, WEDDINGS AND FRONTIERS

In the autumn in Kashgar the Pamirs rarely emerge from behind veils of dust and haze, the exhalation of the desert. In their absence I dreamt of a sedentary life.

It was harvest time. In the fields of Kashgaria women were winnowing in a warm sun, while children bundled and stacked the sheaves of maize. Huge piles of deep yellow cobs stood by the doors of the houses. In the late afternoons I wandered along rural lanes and lay beneath olive trees. Sheep nosed across a field of stubble at my back and a man was carrying pitchforks of hay to where a lane began in pools of shade. Along the road girls in head-scarves and pantaloons were climbing into the trees for walnuts. The field-workers were making their way slowly home, their hoes across their shoulders, clucking cows before them. A man rattled past in a donkey-cart, one hand holding the reins, the other cradling a tiny baby. I envied him. I clung to the last of the light, the last voices dropping through the evening trees, the last figures herding sheep through the ditches. I envied them all, with their attachment to these fields, their sense of belonging. In thrall to this rural idyll, I did not notice cramped lives or a longing for escape.

The next day the haze lifted and I saw the Pamirs for the first time. They were snow-capped and voluptuous. I forgot immediately about the little cottages on the edge of cornfields, the friendly cows, the plump girls in their red kerchiefs.

The mountains were calling.

In Kashgar I sewed Anvar's letters into the lining of my jacket, bought a trilby in the bazaar, and said goodbye to my friends at the Hotel Semen. The bus to Pakistan left from Chini Bagh, the old British Consulate, and customs formalities were performed here as the border posts were remote and unreliable. The passengers were all Pakistani traders returning home with their Chinese loot—thermos flasks, blankets, tea-sets, carpets, silks. Such was the quantity of stuff that there were two buses, one for the passengers and the other, carefully sealed by customs, for the vast and amorphous sacks the Pakistanis liked to call luggage.

Departure was a turbulent affair that dragged on over several hours. In the customs shed the Pakistanis and the Chinese officials screamed abuse at one another in languages that neither understood. Boarding was a dreadful scrum. The Pakistanis become ungovernable when faced with a bus, and the conductor, a stout and increasingly violent Chinese, manhandled them like cattle.

One man had lost his passport, and he and the conductor fought in the aisle, pulling each other's hair. Eventually the conductor managed to throw him off and the bus started. But the passportless Pakistani was indefatigable, and as he ran through the streets of Kashgar behind the bus his friends managed to haul him through a rear window. Other passengers protested, fearful of the delays consequent on having a passportless passenger aboard, and skirmishes broke out between the two factions. Eventually the man was bundled back through the window and dropped into a ditch on the outskirts of town. The issue I noted had divided along tribal lines, Pathans versus Punjabis. The quarrel seemed to put everyone in good spirits. A tape of Pakistani music was put on a new Chinese machine still in its plastic wrappers and a ripple of sweet expectation, a scent of home, ran through the bus.

We stopped for lunch at Upal, a disreputable place full of xenophobes and malcontents. Shoeless young men in patched jackets loitered on the street corners, eyeing us resentfully. Animal carcasses hung outside the eating-houses. Inside squadrons of wasps patrolled the tables. Through the doorway I watched a gang of huge malevolent crows attack a dog cowering in a ditch. Across the road an itinerant magician, with an enraptured audience, was sticking skewers up his nose and swallowing golf balls.

Beyond the town the road climbed beside a wide floodbed where the Ghez river meandered and Bactrian camels grazed amongst the boulders. The valley was framed by foothills, craggy, scarred, and ancient, like petrified dinosaurs. On the far side villages were marked by the yellow blaze of poplars. It was autumn, and it felt good to be on the move. Far ahead the snow peaks were luminous.

The bus was almost entirely male. There was one woman, a Pakistani, and the conductor had placed her next to me knowing that the other men would have protested at having to share a seat with her. She wore a black chador and a red gem in her nose. I was never sure who her husband was. Of the three or four candidates, none behaved as if they had any connection with her.

She was accompanied by her two sons, one about ten and the other perhaps fourteen. The younger boy lay curled in her lap. They spent the whole journey cuddling one another, cooing into each other's necks, their arms entwined. The older boy sat between us. He had graduated from his mother's lap but had not yet joined the intriguing segregated world of the men whom he watched longingly. It seemed curious that his passage through puberty meant the end, not the beginning, of intimacy with women.

It is said that the construction of the Karakoram Highway claimed a life for every mile of roadway. Built jointly by the Chinese and the Pakistanis, it is one of the most spectacular engineering feats of the modern age. It runs from Kashgar to Rawalpindi, a distance of eight hundred miles, over the most difficult mountain terrain in the world. On the Pakistani side alone there are a hundred bridges. It took twenty years to finish, and at any one time as many as 30,000 men were at work on it. The work still goes on, for the mountains seem intent on obliterating this paved upstart. Avalanches, rock falls and subsidence, often stimulated by earthquakes and encroaching glaciers, mean that teams of engineers are constantly working to keep it open.

By late afternoon the valley of the Ghez was narrowing. The river, pressing the road against russet-coloured cliffs, was nibbling at its edges, carrying off chunks of asphalt. In places the cliffs had collapsed, blocking the road with cascades of boulders, some as big as houses. Abandoning the tarmac, vehicles had sought paths over the steep ground above these obstacles.

In a deep gorge between red cliffs we stopped at a checkpoint. While our passports were examined by the Chinese soldiers we crowded into a low windowless hut to escape the wind and to sip bowls of tea. We were among the Kirghiz, and the men squatting by the roadside had bony hawk-nosed faces and wide fur hats. From a high ledge on the far side of the river, the wind-blown silhouettes of three women gazed down on us. While we waited the sun went off the road and we felt ourselves in the grip of a colder, bleaker world. Above us Mount Kongur shone in the last of the light.

After the check-point the road climbed steeply through twisting canyons and tilting fields of boulders. In this bleak landscape the bus had grown cold and silent. At the narrowest passages, the rock faces seemed to scrape the windows. Dusk was falling, and the sky shared its pink glow with the shallows of the river far below us.

Later we emerged in a wide valley, monochrome, treeless and silent. The grey air tasted of stones. We seemed to have passed beyond the frontiers of habitation. Before us the vast Pamir was outlined in ghostly shades. The ashen river had pooled in slate-coloured lakes. Huge grey dunes climbed the flanks of pewter-coloured mountains. Charcoal clouds were riding up from the south. In all this wide and spectacular sweep there was not a single sign of life or of colour save a line of auburn ducks paddling in the cold water beneath us.

An hour or so later the driver stopped and I got down into a biting wind. I planned to stay here for a few days on the shores of Karakul. The Pakistanis, stunned by distance and altitude, pleaded with me to stay on the bus. They peered out through grimy windows at the Roof of the World and shuddered. You can't stop here, they said, waggling their heads in unison. Please, come to Pakistan. I put on a brave face, and waved goodbye. The bus bumped away up the road, its tail-lights winking farewell, then it was gone, curving round the white shoulder of Mount Muztagh.

Karakul means "black lake." It lies in a high pristine valley slung between the shoulders of Mount Kongur and Mount Muztagh. I stumbled down a stony slope and found three bedraggled yurts on the lake shore, a primitive motel. When I called out, a door opened in a long tin shed. A woman haloed by lamplight looked out at me, then slammed the door again. From the shed came desperate wails of laughter.

The staff of this place hadn't seen a guest in weeks. They had been here since April, coming up to these pastures like the spring flocks of sheep. Now, in October, the Pamir had become their prison and they counted the days to season's end and escape. There were four Chinese men and four Turkic women, no longer on speaking terms, a battle of the sexes enlivened with ethnic animosity. The men spent their days lying in their cots, gambling over endless games of cards, getting up only to urinate outside the door. Across the yard the young women had surrendered to hysteria. From their dormitory came gales of violent laughter, verging on tears.

In a blackened kitchen at one end of the shed I found a cook, a local man who had remained neutral in the Battle of Karakul. He was a cheery obliging fellow who came and went unpredictably on a battered bicycle. His hours were so erratic that I took to ordering a meal whenever I chanced to see him. On that first night he concocted a dinner of noodles and dried beef and cabbage which I ate alone at a table in the shed by the light of a hurricane lamp. The wind banged doors and rattled the corrugated sheeting like thunder. Beyond a tin wall was the girls' dormitory. They watched me through peep-holes, sniggering into their hands.

In my yurt, I tried to sleep, fully clothed under five quilts, but the cold kept me awake. I got up and put on another sweater, a coat and a pair of gloves, then dragged the carpet off the floor and slung it over my quilts. I tried to read but the wind crept under the skirts of the yurt and blew my candle out.

In the morning a Kirghiz horseman appeared outside my yurt, materializing from the morning mists to invite me to a wedding. He wore a splendid silver hat like an upturned jelly-mould and carried a shotgun over his shoulder. "Come any time," he barked. "The festivities last for three days." I was delighted to accept. My social calendar in the Chinese Pamirs was relatively empty.

In this remote and silent region the nations and mountains of Central Asia collide. To the west the Pamirs shoulder past the Hindu Kush riding through Afghanistan. To the north the Tien Shan border the new republic of Tadjikistan. To the east the Kunlun Shan march out of China and Tibet towards India and the Himalayas. South lie the Karakorams, the colour of thunder, along Pakistan's frontiers. Few people live here; those that do—Kirghiz and Tadjik nomads—are forever on the move, migrating up and down these cold valleys with the seasons. Marco Polo described them as "out and out bad."

Marco slept at Karakul, *en route* to Cathay, complaining of the cold and the capricious winds. The two great mountains, Kongur and Muztagh Ata, loom at either end of the valley, their summits only rarely emerging from cloud. They never appear together, like two prima donnas unwilling to share the same stage. Both are well over 24,000 feet. If they did not seem higher it was because the lake itself lies at almost half that altitude. The weather here veered between a dazzling brilliance and mist-shrouded gloom, taking the lake from azure blue to lead. Temperatures which fluctuate sixty degrees between the sun and the shade plummet with nightfall. Marriage in such a place becomes an act of survival.

The wedding was in Subash, a summer village to the south of the lake beyond pastures littered with camels, horses, yaks and watercourses. On the way I passed three amorous donkeys. The love-life of donkeys always merits notice. In this *ménage à trois* there was the usual initial uncertainty about who was doing what with whom, but once things were in full swing it was a most remarkable affair. A pair of yaks looked on with what, in the yak world, must pass as unabashed admiration.

I arrived in the village just as two sheep were being slaughtered, and I thought, as their glazed eyes fixed on mine, how strange it was that their last glimpse of the world should be a foreigner in a brown trilby. Despite this shock, they went quietly.

In the village the adobe houses were set apart from one another atop little knolls, like fledgling castles. Dung pats dried on the walls and on the flat roofs emblematic figures stood in silhouette. Yaks sniffed between the houses like tall outlandish dogs and children, their cheeks chapped with cold, chased marbles and each other.

Between the houses and the lake was a collection of yurts where the wedding guests milled about in their finest outfits, swapping salutations and gossip. The women were an exciting splash of colour in this dun-coloured landscape. The married women wore silver jewellery, white wimples and gold teeth. The unmarried women had all turned up in the same outfit. In red jackets, crimson skirts and scarlet headscarves, they were as happily uniform as stockbrokers.

The men's clothes were more eclectic. Bits of old Mao suits, tweed jackets and overcoats which would have cut a dash in a Chicago speakeasy were accompanied by silk sashes, tall boots and the jelly-mould hats. Their faces were whiskery and shrewd and dark as walnuts.

On the plain beyond the village, *buzkashi* had begun. The game is the ancestor of polo, played with a dead goat rather than a ball. There are no rules and no teams; it is every man for himself. With their whips in their teeth, the riders try to manoeuvre their mounts through the scrum of horses, leaning down amid the stamping hooves to pluck the carcass from the ground. When one succeeds in lifting it the chase is on, and wild galloping charges sweep back and forth across the plain as the riders try to wrest the goat from one another. Having done so, they score by dropping it into a circle of stones. Originally the game was played with a dead man, a prisoner-of-war or someone equally dispensable. Older enthusiasts bemoan the substitution of a goat carcass, the way elderly members might decry the one-day game over drinks in the bar at Lord's.

Back on the lake shore the speeches were under way. At Kirghiz weddings they have the novelty of being sung. With two attendants the groom was singing his way towards married life—a dirge-like tune—as he slowly approached the bride's house surrounded by the vast wedding party. He was a bit of a heart-throb, tall and bashfully handsome. His cashmere overcoat and high-heeled boots marked him out as a man who was not short of a sheep or two.

It was more difficult to form an opinion of the bride. She emerged from the house under a red blanket like an accused prisoner. Her attendants ushered her out to stand beside her betrothed while the best man began his peroration from the back of a donkey-cart. This was sung as well, with improvised verses about the groom which had his audience slapping each other with hilarity. When it was over, the bride was hustled away again, still under her blanket. Later someone told me that the groom had paid a bride price of ten camels and twenty goats, a figure that was considered dangerously inflationary.

The *buzkashi* players rode up like a victorious army, horses and riders snorting and breathing hard. I found myself swept into one of the yurts in their midst. We sat round in a crosslegged circle and merrily ate balls of rancid yak butter. The horsemen were in the kind of high spirits that one would expect of men who had spent the last hour engaged in ritualized warfare.

"What are weddings like in your country?" one man asked.

The butter made speech difficult. "Similar sort of thing," I managed at last. "Less butter, more cake." Unaccountably they thought this hilarious, and thumped me on the back, which proved a great aid to digestion.

"Do you play *buzkashi* in your country?" one asked, his face still flushed from the game. I tried to explain about polo but they quickly recognized it as a sport for wimps.

From sport the conversation turned to geopolitics. They were uncertain about England's whereabouts but agreed it lay somewhere to the north of Kashgar. Did England too belong to China they wanted to know. I said it didn't but parts of China had belonged to England. They glanced at each other out of the corners of their eyes. I was obviously a braggart and a fool.

After a time the main course arrived: grilled mutton atop huge plates of pilau, washed down with bowls of sour milk. Later we staggered outside for the dancing. Night had fallen and the lake was brimming with moonlight. Cold constellations hung between the snow peaks. The musicians played three-stringed lutes and whining flutes which set the sheep running for cover. Men and women danced in segregated lines, their arms round each other's shoulders in the manner of drunken football supporters. Beneath the icy face of Muztagh Ata we seemed at last to have escaped the foxtrot. At midnight antique trucks arrived to carry the revellers home to outlying encampments, their headlights dancing away into the darkness.

I made my way back across the dark plain to my yurt, the sound of flutes trailing at my heels. Horses and Bactrian camels were grazing in corridors of moonlight. I gave the yaks a wide berth. They have an evil reputation and are said to hate Europeans.

The following afternoon I heard the bus from Kashgar long before it reached Karakul, a distant whine amid silent mountains. I packed my bag and trudged up to the road. When the wheezing vehicle hove into view I flagged it down. This was the last request stop in the Chinese Pamirs.

On the bus I found the Pakistanis at prayer. The murmur of *"Allah Akbar"* passed up and down the aisle as the faithful bowed in unison in their seats. I took a place next to a bedraggled purple turban bumping the back of the seat in front of him. After prayers my new neighbour, full of the grace of Allah, shared his meagre dinner of raisins and bread with me, then enquired after the whereabouts of Salman Rushdie. When I protested ignorance, he only smiled, waggled his head, and nudged me in the ribs. "Come, come," he said as if he knew I was keeping poor Salman in my spare bedroom, "I am telling no one. Allah be my witness."

The bus had the ventilation of an open truck. Mountain winds from the summit of Muztagh Ata howled in through ill-fitting windows and gaps in the floorboards. The Pakistanis wrapped their heads in towels and went to sleep. I scratched a hole in the frost and peered out on a dim white world. We were climbing into higher and higher valleys, empty in the moonlight. All around us were ghostly peaks. The stars were few but spectacularly bright, as if the cold had extinguished all but the best.

Somewhere around midnight we blew a tire. The driver and the better-clad passengers got down to fix it by torchlight. There was no jack but we managed to lever the axle and cram boulders beneath it. The cold was so fierce that we worked in shifts, retreating to the unheated bus to warm ourselves. All about us were indifferent mountains armoured with snow.

We arrived at Tashkurgan at 2 a.m., and tramped into a dark hotel clad inside and out with bright yellow tiles. I slept fully dressed beneath a quilt as thick as a yak's coat in a room cloudy with my own breath. In the morning the attendants came down the tiled corridors with huge bunches of keys unlocking the doors. Downstairs in the lobby we found the receptionist dressed in a fur coat. She was seated in an armchair staring at the wall. Pakistanis queued to yell in her ear—"tea, tea"—but she did not respond, as if she had frozen solid during the night. She was a runaway winner for that most fiercely contested of prizes: the Most Miserable Hotel Receptionist in China.

Almost two thousand years ago Ptolemy identified Tashkurgan as the gateway to Seres, the Land of Silk. The various branches of the Silk Road—those coming from the west through Samarkand and Afghanistan and those coming up from India—converged here. One gets the sense it hasn't changed much in the intervening centuries. There is a single street with a collection of ramshackle tea-houses and blacksmiths. Horses are hitched to the telegraph poles and the suburbs are tents. The population, chiefly Tadjiks, are watched over by an uneasy Chinese garrison. Travellers still complain of the cold, the poor food, the vast distances, and the altitude.

While the Pakistanis crowded into a tea-shop opposite the hotel, I went up the road to look at the ruined fort, a confusion of rubble and battlements. Outside an eating-house a tethered goat, awaiting the butcher, was enjoying its last meal, a pair of baggy underpants. Schoolgirls in scarlet jackets and skirts giggled as I passed. Loudspeakers in the trees started to broadcast, the usual rousing music interspersed with patronizing advice and snippets of good news. Mercifully it was all in Chinese, a language few understood here.

The bus started in mid morning. The Pakistanis, full of tea and warm nan, were in high spirits. Today they would be home. My neighbour, who seemed to have forgotten my part in sheltering Salman Rushdie, wrote his address in my notebook and demanded that I come to visit him in Peshawar. His home was my home, he insisted. He would get me a Kalashnikov. "Boom, boom, boom," he cried. "No trouble."

Beyond Tashkurgan the empty road rose through wide valleys gilded with yellow pastures. In local languages *pamir* means pasture, and the passes through these mountains are a series of broad grassy valleys rising between high peaks. Sir Aurel Stein dismissed the Khunjerab Pass as "an excursion for ladies." Spectacular switchbacks may be rare but Khunjerab has its own difficulties. The name means "Bloody Valley," which may refer to the Wakhi and Hunza bandits who preyed upon caravans in days gone by, or to the habit of muleteers of stabbing the muzzles of their horses with spikes to ease their breathing in this rarified atmosphere. When the Karakoram Highway crosses its apex at 15,528 feet, it is the highest public road in the world.

We passed a caravanserai said to contain the skeletons of an unknown army. Yurts were dotted here and there in the vast valleys, sheltering in hollows. In the scattered villages horses were parked outside the houses and huge mastiffs wearing spiked collars to ward off wolves slept in the sun on doorsteps. Himalayan marmots sat up in the plain and scented the morning. A blue river tumbled between blond grasses. Frozen sheets of water lay between the meadows where horses in quilted blankets grazed. A herd of yaks stampeded off the road like sheep as we approached. Once I saw a young girl in red tripping down a track carrying two buckets, gloveless, the icy water slopping over the rims and splashing round her feet. In this lonely place this small figure had the dramatic effect of a carnival parade.

Afghanistan now lay only a few miles to the west. A caravan of laden camels came down the pass, treading as softly as birds with their big padded feet. We passed an army post forlornly flying a red flag. Beyond a vale of downy meadow littered with snow we emerged, at the very end of China, in a bowl of yellow and red grasses beneath an assembly of magnificent snow peaks gathering thunder clouds. The road climbed its north rim to the watershed and the frontier.

At the top the bus stopped, and we got out to gaze back into China, back down the long pamirs to the distant army post, its red flag an insignificant fleck of colour in the clear majesty of this place. The mountains glittered and the earth fell away on all sides. I felt dizzy with delight, but it might have been the altitude.

On the bus my neighbour had collapsed in his seat, green and unconscious. We were three miles above sea level.

On the far side of the pass we fell into Pakistan as into a deep well, the road plummeting down a heart-stopping switchback. In a moment it seemed we were in the Karakorams, a name which means "black crumbling rock." We dropped between dark peaks into a gorge cut by the Khunjerab river, full of snow and fans of gravel, the residue of rock slides. Sheer rock faces pressed around the road which twisted heroically in this confinement, looking for escape. I craned my neck at the windows, trying to catch a glimpse of the peaks far above us. Occasionally the sun found its way into the gorge and the dark walls and the river suddenly sparkled.

After a time the river grew banks, and the banks grew small trees in autumn colours. Finally the gorge widened into a valley and we arrived at the town of Sust. At the customs shed a Pakistani soldier came on board, very smart in pressed flannels, military sweater and beret. *"Salaam aleikum,"* he boomed. *"Waleikum salaam,"* chorused the bus. We got down into a happy scrum of greeting. "How do you do, sir," said the immigration officer. "Delighted to see you."

After months of the alien difficulties of China, Pakistan seemed like paradise. I had crossed the Roof of the World and suddenly found myself among people who spoke English, took milk in their tea and knew the latest cricket results.

Thirteen

THE SACRED ROCKS OF HUNZA

Had the major been born in another era, he would almost certainly have been murdered. A century ago patricide and fratricide were absolutely *de rigueur* among the ruling families of Hunza and Nagar. Questions of succession were invariably resolved with a blood-bath, and family gatherings tended to be uneasy affairs where the men sat about the palace smiling broadly at each other, their coats bulging with weaponry, their retainers saddling the horses for a quick getaway.

In the modern world tradition counts for nothing, and I found the major in an apricot orchard in Gulmit feeding biscuits to his King Charles spaniel. He was one of the many younger sons of the former Mir, or ruler, of Hunza. Now retired from the Pakistani army, he had come up from Gilgit on his autumn visit, and was installed in the old inn overlooking the polo field which, typically of Hunza, doubles as the village square.

The major wore a cravat, a cardigan, and a pencil moustache. He was a man of the most impeccable manners. He rang for tea and we chatted about Virgil. Beyond the orchard wall the valley fell through neat terraced fields to where the canyon of the Hunza river cleaved the Karakorams. Autumn leaves fell about our ears. I asked him about the polo ground where school-children and calves were trailing across the midfield.

"The last time a match was played here," he mused, "must have been about '62 or '63. A number of us rode up from Baltit; no highway in those days, of course. The Mir was still in residence here. With so many horses about, we decided to have a knock. Someone was badly thrown, I remember. One of my brothers, I think."

The major was a man of eclectic tastes and interests. He was a great admirer of Omar Khayyám, the Renaissance, Joanna Lumley, and Brian Johnston's cricket commentaries. When Joanna Lumley had visited Hunza some years ago he had been delegated to escort her around. One learnt to keep him off the topic. She inspired in him tireless rhapsody.

"So elegant," he sighed. "Always so polite, and always elegant. Do you know Joanna?"

Like most people in the Northern Areas he spoke of Pakistanis as if they belonged to another country. "We are not Pakistanis," Hunzakuts said, as others might say "We are not thieves or wife-beaters." The major was scathing about the government, the influence of the Muslim parties, and the hypocrisy of the ban on alcohol. Hunza is famous for its "Hunza water," a home-brew made from mulberries.

"Here in Hunza we are more enlightened about these matters," he said. "We make a little wine to take with dinner. That is all." The major was a great champion of individual conscience. "We are Ismailis, followers of the Aga Khan, and we are progressive people, not a rabble like the Paksitanis."

After dinner I found him morose in the moonlight, his breath smelling of mulberries. The enlightenment of the afternoon was already a memory. "Do you know the trouble with the people of Hunza?" he demanded. "They are drunkards. Feeble-minded." He grew maudlin. "We are so fortunate to have the great Imam, the Aga Khan, to tell us what to do."

The major gazed across the valley at moonlit mountains, and began to quote Omar Khayyám, something about filling wine cups, and not worrying about tomorrow or yesterday.

"It would be easier to live for the day," he declared, "if we only had some inkling of the morrow. So many opportunities we let pass because we think others might come along."

I presumed he was still thinking about Joanna.

Hunza is a quite remarkable little kingdom, a miniature Switzerland without the traditions of tolerance or good timekeeping. Barely sixty miles long, it boasts three separate languages. It shares its valley with Nagar, which lies on the opposite bank of the river. The two peoples, within shouting distance of each other, have been conducting a murderous feud for the better part of four hundred years, though the modern age, which came to Hunza about twenty years ago, has seen an uneasy truce. When they weren't setting about their neighbours, the Hunzakuts made a living from the merchants who picked their precarious way through the mountain passes along this branch of the Silk Road. They didn't bother with toll charges. It was simpler to plunder the caravans, keep the goods, and sell the traders into slavery.

Before the building of the Karakoram Highway in the 1970s the only access to Hunza and Nagar was along a precipitous track that had hardly been upgraded since the days of Alexander the Great. Colonel Biddulph, visiting the area in 1876, described the Hunza Road as the "most difficult and dangerous" in the Himalayas. In places it was little more than a ledge a few inches wide. Coming up from Gilgit, where the sheer cliffs press in on the river gorge, a staggering series of hairpins and zig-zags carried the track from the water's edge to dizzy heights and back down again in search of a way forward. When nothing else would do, galleries were cut into the sheer cliff or wooden scaffolding erected. In the narrowest places horses had to be lowered by ropes steadied by men hanging on to their tails. Baggage animals were out of the question, and goods were carried in and out of this little country by porters.

One of the difficulties the British had in dealing with Hunza was that the remoteness of the place had bred delusions of grandeur in the Mir. He believed his tiny kingdom to be the equal of China, and likened himself to Alexander the Great, from whom he claimed descent. When the British first arrived at the end of the last century, he took them for petitioners seeking to make Queen Victoria his vassal. Not wishing to waste any time, the British deposed him, replacing him with a more amenable stepbrother whom the Mir had carelessly neglected to murder on his way to the throne.

A boy fetched the keys for the Mir's old residence from the house next door, as if the neighbours had been asked to pop in now and again. It was a shambling wooden pile with fireplaces set athwart the corners and little wall cupboards with glass doors and narrow shelves. The only litter was forty-year-old numbers of *Punch*. In the cobwebbed cellars I found a rusty tin of butterscotch topping and an old box of seeds from Henry Sutton, Great Yarmouth.

In the town museum, a dusty room on the other side of the polo field, there were nineteenth-century trunks, like those still made in the bazaars of Kashgar, a stuffed snow leopard whose tail had fallen off and been swept into a corner, a variety of ghastly-looking weapons which the Hunzakuts used to try out on visitors, and an American Smith & Wesson rifle, which had been presented to the Mir by Lord Kitchener in 1903.

Arriving from China, one had the sense of having crossed a great divide. But the difficulties of the old Hunza Road were such that the people of Upper Hunza had more contact with the Tadjiks across the Khunjerab Pass than with the people a few miles downstream who were destined to become fellow Pakistanis. Most of the items in the museum were wedding gifts from China that arrived with brides from the kingdom of Sarikol at Tashkurgan a century ago. Silk gowns and waistcoats hung on nails in the walls. My guide, a dark-eyed girl who was another descendant of the Mir, modelled them for me, parading glamorously in the cramped room, until I began to feel like a long-suffering husband attendant on his wife's shopping expedition.

The major gave me a lift down the valley to Baltit. Trails of stones ran down from the heights above us to bounce across the road and disappear over the edge into the river below. Had we been unlucky, boulders would have followed. The chief cause of traffic accidents on the Karakoram Highway is speeding rocks. Local people believe that the continual problem of avalanche has been greatly worsened by the road-building methods of the Chinese. Apparently the inventors of gunpowder never moved a boulder that they could blow up, and their enthusiasm for pyrotechnics has unsettled the whole region.

The road changed everything, the major said. Twenty years ago Hunza was one of the most isolated places in Asia. The people lived at the bottom of a deep well and had little contact with the outside world. Now with the Karakoram Highway they are up and down to Gilgit every week. Development has come to the most remote villages. Twenty years ago daughters were never educated. Now, said the major, 99 percent of girls are at school and 100 percent of boys.

It was an echo of the Silk Road. Round the Taklamakan the old road had brought to the most remote oases the explosive impact of new ideas, from Buddhism to underground irrigation to the foxtrot. The story of development in Central Asia was the story of journeys. The moment someone started packing their bags, change was afoot.

I took Hunza for paradise. It was autumn. The days were bright and warm, and the nights were cold. The orchards, full of magpies and girls in red smocks, had turned the colour of ripening fruit, and the poplars trembled and showered leaves like gold dust. Across the valley the great Rakaposhi, towards which all the houses of Hunza were orientated, unfurled banners of cloud from its snowy shoulders. On dark nights the lights of Nagar were a fallen constellation.

I walked for days in this landscape of steep terraced villages, autumn colours and mountain peaks. I walked without destination, climbing at will through rose-hips and wild herbs and boulders and fields so steep the farmers were planting winter wheat on their hands and knees. Mountain shepherds were my guides. "Scrambly, scrambly," they warned about the more difficult paths.

For all its grandeur it was a landscape of surprising intimacy. Perspectives were continually shifting. Whole mountains vanished in the turn of a path. Another turn would reveal an unsuspected village hidden in the fold of a familiar view. Sometimes, alone on remote paths, I was greeted by voices and had to search for their owners, finding them on a roof looking down through trees or in a field at my feet.

I slept in mountain huts and lunched on dried mulberries. I walked up to the meadows beneath Ultar Glacier in a amphitheatre of peaks. Above me the sheer face of Ultar Peak, one of the highest unclimbed mountains in the world, rose more than two and a half miles into a grey mist from which bright snowflakes drifted down into the sunlight. I walked to Altit where sheep were munching their way through fallen leaves in the orchard beneath the fort. Its rambling rooms were full of old hay and carved Tibetan pillars. Beneath bowers of yellowing leaves I climbed lanes of soft dust to stone villages where the roofs were carpets of drying apricots and the water-channels were gurgling with creamy water.

In the late afternoons I dropped down the steep slopes to stroll home along the highway. There was little traffic on the KKH. In this vertical landscape it offers a flat and open space that has been absorbed into local life as a public square. Young men stroll along it in the evening hand-in-hand. Boys were playing cricket, arguing over who was Imran Khan. A girl, driving her goats home, met another going in the other direction, and for a moment there was gridlock on the Karakoram Highway, a traffic jam of goats. In the dying light children stood along the tops of orchard walls solemnly waving to me, waving goodbye as if my passage was inevitably a departure.

Below Baltit by the highway are the Sacred Rocks of Hunza, a stone "guest book" where visitors through the centuries have carved their names. Many are in Chinese characters. The latest were left by the workers on the Karakoram Highway. The earliest names were the pioneers of the Silk Road, Chinese pilgrims who came to India in search of Buddhist scriptures. Entranced by this landscape, I found it odd that these travel-worn figures, hurrying home with news of nirvana, did not lift their heads long enough from the hard road to see paradise all about them here in Hunza. Perhaps they did, but recognized it was not a paradise in which they belonged.

I caught the bus down the valley to Gilgit. It was the odalisque of the bus world: exotic, colourful, curvaceous, less a bus than an escaped fairground ride. The driver brayed with delight on the worst corners. The road was a roller-coaster, and the giddy passengers joked and held hands while we skidded round hairpin bends, inches from oblivion, our coloured lights flashing and our horn playing a tune.

Gilgit was a raffish town where all the hill tribes of northern Pakistan jostled uneasily on narrow pavements. Mountains loomed in the suburbs. Forlorn cows wandered the streets like lost children and the traffic policemen fell asleep at their posts. In the evenings the electric light was fitful and the shopkeepers depended on candles and gas lanterns. I lodged in a hotel where the overgrown gardens were deep in autumn leaves, the bungalows had the fusty air of rooms unopened for years and blue-tits nested in the lavatories.

It was the beginning of November and Gilgit was in the throes of its annual polo tournament, the most glamorous of sporting fixtures, a cross between Wimbledon and the Cup Final. Teams had come from all over the Northern Areas with their horses, their retainers and their retinue of fans. Matches were played every day at 2 p.m. in the polo ground beyond the mosque. Rakaposhi overlooked the ground with the same reassuring familiarity as the gasometers at the Oval.

By the gateway a plaque inscribed with the lines of J.K. Stephens struck a note in keeping with the grandiose setting:

Let other people play at other things,
The king of games is still the game of kings.

Stabled at the town barracks, the teams rode through the streets to the ground every afternoon. Many were local teams from Daiynor, and from Gilgit town, but the best tended to have some form of official sponsorship. Northern Light Infantry, the successor to the Gilgit Scouts, fielded a fine squad, and one of the best teams was the romantically named Northern Areas Public Works Department.

The terraces were a broad cement wall round the ground from which the more enthusiastic fans spilled down onto the touch-line. A dignitary threw out the first ball from the canopied seats above the centre-line. On the first afternoon the dignitary was a little old man, as wizened as dried fruit. Someone said he was the Mir of Nagar. He wore a safari hat, a tweed coat too big for him and trousers hitched above his delicate ankles. All through the match he cadged cigarettes from his neighbours and found difficulty in staying awake.

In polo in Pakistan only one rule appears to be generally agreed upon: goals must be scored between the goal posts. For the rest, it is a free-for-all. Much of the play involves impeding one's opponent, hooking his stick, charging him off the ball. It seems to be only the vaguest kind of gentleman's agreement that keeps the players from murdering one another. The game resembles a medieval battle: dust and horses and masculine pride all brought together in a fearful jumble. Throughout the play musicians keep up a swirling barrage of music with whining flutes and thundering drums. Goals are greeted with terrific crescendos, a sort of crazed fanfare. The music, old hands say, is for the horses. It gees them up.

The riders were all fine fellows, athletic and competitive, but the horses were the heroes of the game. They played the whole match without change, at a pace that makes English polo seem positively pedestrian. Wheeling from end to end, lathered with sweat, their mouths flecking foam, they were tough and tireless. They were horses to dream about.

Cup Final Day at the end of the week dawned clear and crisp. The ground were packed, the musicians all wore white, and the players arrived, for the first time, in knee pads and hard hats. It was Northern Light Infantry versus the Public Works Department. I met the major in the crowds and he shook my hand until my arm rattled. The excitement had rendered him speechless.

From the opening strike, no quarter was given. Players marked each other closely and the battle to get on the ball was fierce. Galloping horses rode into each other in midfield or, chasing wide passes, rode full tilt into the crowds. There were a couple of nasty falls and a spectator was taken away with a bleeding head. In the mêlée of jostling horses polo sticks were wielded like scythes. When they broke, boys ran onto the pitch with replacements.

At half-time the grooms walked the horses round the centre circle. A woman next to me said to her companion: "They really are the most exquisite creatures. They are like gods."

In the second half, with an inspired performance by their centre forward, a black stallion with a star on its forehead, Northern Light Infantry made a late surge that had the Public Works Department defence floundering. They won 9–6. At the final whistle the musicians marched onto the pitch playing wildly, the winning team danced in the centre circle, their arms round each other's shoulders, and the cheering crowds were lathicharged by policemen by way of celebration.

In all this excitement the horses were forgotten. While the stadium cheered and danced, the grooms led them away unnoticed, through the gate and out into the empty streets where they clattered on the pavements, lifting their feet awkwardly like dancers on high heels. I followed after them, wondering what it was that was so emotive about them. The horses hung their heads as if finally admitting exhaustion. Trailing home to stables and oats, they seemed infinitely sad. Perhaps it was the funereal image of a procession of riderless horses, or the sounds of cheering, laughter in another room.

When the ancient Chinese dreamt of horses, they dreamt of journeys, of crossing frontiers. When they built a Wall, they wanted the inviolability of home. The Wall was never a great success, if only because the world was full of horsemen. Perhaps the horses were not a great success either, but they were such a pretty notion. One could not help but be seduced by them. Trailing after them through the streets of Gilgit, I clung to the dream of horses though it felt at times like unrequited love.

Fourteen

TEA WITH MOHAMMED

Mr Mohammed Mohammed sat all day in the upstairs lobby of the hotel like a minor potentate holding court. Shuttered against the heat, the room was suffused with a watery light. Through the day a trickle of visitors swam in and out to pay their respects. In the evening Mr Mohammed Mohammed descended the stairs with a walking-stick and the air of a departing diva to a waiting taxi.

We took afternoon tea together, a ritual he insisted should include toffees and decorative bowls of rose petals.

"Shall I be mother?" Mr Mohammed Mohammed poured. The muffled sounds of Rawalpindi—the cries of hawkers, the car horns, the horses' hooves—wafted up to us like voices from another world.

Mr Mohammed Mohammed was a charming fellow with a splendid handlebar moustache and a wicked smile. His size—he must have been two hundred and fifty pounds—served to give him presence but also a remarkable delicacy. He served tea and distributed biscuits with precise and dainty movements.

He knew about the English and understood the importance of placing me, socially. At first he was disappointed to learn that my ancestry did not include any members of the House of Lords. I was redeemed however from social ignominy by my grandfather, who had raised cattle. Mr Mohammed Mohammed had the highest regard for the British cow. He had been to England, knew Heathrow well, and had once taken a bus to Oxford. "So beautiful. Really it was like being in a colour television. The cows were so clean." With the cows, my stock rose considerably.

As an older man Mr Mohammed Mohammed felt it incumbent upon him to offer the occasional piece of advice. He liked to direct my explorations around the town, and tried to warn me about the intricacies of Pakistani customs. One afternoon he told me I must grow a moustache. My face, he declared, was crying for a moustache. His own was a luxuriant affair, standing out from his cheeks like a cat's whiskers to guide him through doorways.

In a land of serious moustaches, Rawalpindi is in a league of its own. It is the headquarters of the Pakistan army, and where the military traditions of the Raj meet Pathan *machismo,* the handlebar, the pencil-thin, the Manchu, and the rare but splendid Salvador Dali flourish in such profusion that the clean-shaven male feels naked, and not a little plain.

Rawalpindi is the kind of town whose glorious assault on the senses makes newcomers to the subcontinent swoon. Pakistani trucks, as ornate as bordellos, are famous but the same gaiety touches everything from breakfast stalls to dentists' surgeries. The former are shining mosaics of flattened cola tins while the latter are plastered with garish posters of smiling faces, their cheeks peeled away to reveal rows of perfect white molars. The venerable Morris Minor is barely recognizable here, suddenly the ageing gigolo of the motor world, kitted out with flame decals, tasselled sunshades and horns that play "Land of Hope and Glory."

In the narrow streets of the Rajah bazaar the tradesmen are incapable of selling anything without first rendering it decorative. The drink stands are adorned with row on row of polished fruit like coloured bulbs on amusement rides. Banners of gaudy cloth are interlaced like tapestries in front of the tailors. The spice merchants sculpt their wares into tall pyramids of colour—deep saffron, burgundy chilli powders, the pale green of ground cumin. The ginger sellers construct high curving walls of the knobbly roots. Regiments of sheep's heads, bleached and hairless, gazed up at me in perfect formation. At the next stall their hearts, still pink and moist, were laid out in a herringbone pattern.

The crowds that swept through these alleys were as exhilarating as the goods. The women, when they abandoned the black chador, wore colours that would panic the faint-hearted. Veils and scarves, meant for secrecy, became just another form of adornment. The men, hawk-faced beneath ramshackle turbans, wore cloaks and ancient Enfield rifles.

Beyond, in the warren of medieval alleys, the tall ancient houses spilled rich smells, noise and people into the streets. An old man on a rope bed ordered scented tea for me while gangs of children pursued each other around corners. A wedding turned into the street, the groom in a plumed turban, gold curved slippers, garlands of flowers and tinsel, the bride in a sack.

To the south the streets of Saddar Bazaar disgorge into the Mall, a long colonial thoroughfare that once carried the Grand Trunk Road through the city towards the Khyber Pass. Here Rawalpindi pauses for breath. A sign in reception in Flashman's Hotel asks guests to leave their weapons at the desk before entering the restaurant. Next door is a parish church lifted from the Home Counties, the caretaker dressed like a showy apostle. From across the road, among the lengthening shadows on the green, came the sound of leather on willow.

Rawalpindi adjoins the country's capital, Islamabad, a new creation begun in the 1950s. Islamabad is the embodiment of the idea that capitals are inevitably divorced from the countries they rule. It is a triumph of the urban planner, posed over his drawing-board with T-square and rule. Sectioned and subsectioned, districts and streets are identified by numbers as if they were experiments—G-8, F-1 and so on. In its grid of tree-lined avenues, where auto-rickshaws and horse-drawn tongas are banned, the suburban houses are said to be modelled on those of Texas. The "bazaars" are shopping malls. For the devotee of indigenous architecture it is a nightmare. One returns to the spirited idiosyncracies of 'Pindi with a sense of relief.

But appearances can deceive. Islamabad may be the sterile architecture of the suburbs but the life-blood of Pakistani society—gossip and scandal—thrives behind its twitching curtains with a metropolitan vigour.

Over tea Mr Mohammed Mohammed and I read the reports of the latest scandals in the morning papers with the loyalty of soap opera addicts. Members of the government, it was alleged, had been visiting a brothel in F-10. Political argument turned on whether the madam was in the pay of the opposition party. Mr Mohammed Mohammed was both shocked and impressed—shocked by the hypocrisy of the politicians, some of whom advocated Islamic law, and impressed that female escorts could be procured for as little as 1,000 rupees.

"If Sharia law demands the amputation of a hand for the crime of theft," Mr Mohammed Mohammed wondered, "what is the penalty for fornication?"

"Pakistan has become so petty and narrow-minded," he sighed. "It was not always so. Once we were a more worldly people. You must go to law Taxila. It was a city of the world."

I went by train and breakfasted in the station dining-room on white linen beneath big-bladed fans. The waiter was a garrulous fellow with stained teeth and the hands of a mechanic. I was the only diner so he joined me for toast, eventually showing me his two prize possessions: an honourable discharge from the Libyan army and a Birmingham bus pass.

The scattered ruins of Taxila lie to the west of Rawalpindi in the lee of the Muree Hills. Astride Asia's greatest trade routes, most notably the Silk

Road, it was one of the most cosmopolitan cities of its age, flourishing two thousand years ago. Asoka, the great unifier of India, was Viceroy here in the third century BC. Alexander, pushing towards the Indian Ocean, garrisoned the city with Macedonians. Arrian, Strabo and Plutarch wrote of its beauty and its wealth. St. Thomas turned up to preach the Gospel while the great Chinese pilgrims came looking for Buddhist scriptures. Its religious establishments ranged from Greek temples to Zoroastrian temples to Christian churches to Buddhist shrines. Few cities in Asia so represent the different cultural currents that crossed and recrossed the continent.

It was destroyed by nomads. Late in the fifth century, the White Huns swept across Gandhara and the Punjab. When Xuan Zang arrived in Taxila 150 years later he found the city had never really recovered.

The ancient highways of Asian trade have been replaced by a branch railway line serviced by an antiquated steam train. Between pastures of white buffalo and a green river the wooden carriages swayed like ships. Two soldiers holding hands rode shotgun while the guards paraded the country platforms in immaculate white uniforms like extras hoping to catch the eye of a producer. The only other passengers were a family of four munching their way through baskets of cold chicken. The mother was a tented figure peering out at the world through a screened visor. Her drumsticks were posted through a handy flap.

Taxila station slept in the midst of corn fields. In the forecourt the horses of the tonga taxis were at lunch in their nosebags while their drivers dozed in the upholstered seats. Up the road I found a small but splendid museum full of finds from the ancient city. Here the earliest Buddhas were entirely Hellenistic, vigorous figures with flowing locks and moustaches that would still cut a dash in 'Pindi. Later the image became icon, serene and stylized, keeping his own counsel beneath lowered lids.

A second-century BC coin had Plato ill-at-ease in a tin helmet. Another showed the King of Kabul like a young Alexander. Stone reliefs of dancing scenes bore fragments of big-breasted women with hour-glass figures, stripped to the waist. I glanced over my shoulder to find the guard leering.

Outside in the gardens rose petals floated in the fountain and rooks had colonized the cedar trees. I waded through long grass and dancing crickets to the ruins of Sirkap where the excavated main street, an avenue two thousand years old, was as broad and straight as any in Islamabad. All that remained of the houses were their foundations. I wandered through vanished rooms.

The ruins of Taxila are spread across a wide area, and I walked between the sites along country lanes where men in cloaks ride Chinese bicycles and caryatid women carry jars of water with the posture of dancers. Tea-shops crop up at convenient intervals. In one a local dignitary bought my round. At a signal from the great man a boy, singing in a nearby orchard, ran up to fill my pockets with tangerines.

On the roadside I met a beekeeper selling bottles of honey. He was a morose figure seated monkishly on a rope bed outside his tent. Custom was slow, but then he was not a man for the hard sell. Bearded and intense, he rocked back and forth reciting the Koran, haunted by the spectre of sin. His honey was called Sweet Desires.

At the temple of Jaulian above fields of stacked corn the courts were full of birdsong. The guard was a cringing figure obsessed with damnation. He showed me the people of Atlantis, rows of tormented souls on the lower registers of the stupa, and warned me against fornication. He pointed out two women, one Greek and one Chinese, hovering at the shoulders of the seated Buddha like angels. "Temptresses," he hissed, "trying to distract his meditation."

On the way to Mohra Moradu I met a party of schoolboys going home along lanes of white dust. Their uniforms consisted of grey chalwar chemises and black berets. Wooden writing boards hung from their belts. They were boisterous and good-natured and inquisitive. At their centre was a blind boy, as alert and slight as a gazelle, his face tilted upwards, listening. Pushing forward, he seized my hand and without a word led me along paths, never hesitating in his darkness.

Beyond the village we rose through the gorge of Meri where the late sun was trickling between the olive trees. The boy never let go my hand, plunging determinedly onwards, stumbling from time to time on the uneven path, but never faltering. His other hand groped in front of him, feeling the air. He reminded me of the girl in Yingda, skipping along the raised causeways to her horses. He had the same ethereal quality, as if later I might wonder if I had imagined him.

He led me round the curve of the gorge to where the ruined monastery of Mohra Moradu appeared suddenly, nestling between hills, hidden from the wider valley in a leafy glen. Here in an open court enclosed by stone walls and heavy boughs he dropped my hand at last, a signal of arrival.

Neither the White Huns nor the long centuries had disturbed the sense of sanctuary here. The lines of grey stone, the birdsong, the stillness, the lengthening shadows have created a refuge. On the swept gravel of the courts I left a trail of footprints, and knew that by tomorrow some custodian would have brushed them away.

The blind boy inhabited this place like a sprite, a reincarnate monk, flitting through the arches, beneath the varnished porticoes. He had forgotten me. He vanished in the monks' cells, reappeared round one of the stupas, running his hand over the tiered figures, then darted away again towards the refectory. Once I saw him run into a wall, and he stopped, suddenly surprised by this miscalculation.

The figures of the great stupa are composed and assured, dressed in robes whose draperies are executed in the finest Hellenistic tradition. Dreamy celestial figures emerge from the clouds round the heads of the Buddhas. I imagined the pilgrims' perambulations, walking round and round these stupas as the Tibetans had done at Xiahe, prayer weighted with the symbolism of travel, like the characters of Chinese opera signifying long journeys by walking in circles.

Later I followed the water channels and goat tracks back towards the road. The call of the muezzin was floating across the valley, beckoning people home, and the shadows were lengthening in the dusty lanes. I turned to see the blind boy standing on a rise above the village, a thin wraith, his head cocked. He knew the whole landscape before him. He could see it all, the warren of lanes and paths, the herdsmen as they brought their cattle down from the hills calling to one another, the haystacks with their scent of fermenting grass. But he could not see me. In this wide place I was invisible to him, the one thing that did not belong.

At the station the evening was smoky and full of bats. From the train I gazed across darkening fields where russet strips of sky shone in the irrigation ditches.

In Rawalpindi the hotel lobby was empty; Mr Mohammed Mohammed had already gone home. Early the next morning I flew to England. In London in an empty house I sat for a time with my bag still packed, waiting for the journey to end, for things to come to rest. I thought of Fu Wen in the mosque in Xi'an, her head tilting towards me in a twilight of crickets. I could hear her voice, her regrets about departure.

When darkness came I got up, turned on the light at my desk and unpacked my notebooks. On the first page I found Wang, dancing alone in his corridor of sun.

STANLEY STEWART

was a member of the Persian Royal Road Expedition whose work was chron-
icled in a series of television films. He has also been a farmer in
Tuscany, a fisherman off the coast of Ireland, a film cameraman in Turkey
and Iran, and an erector of circus tents. He is the author of *Old Serpent Nile,*
an account of his journey to the source of the river. He is also a regular con-
tributor to *The Sunday Times* and *The Daily* and *Sunday Telegraph.* He was
born in Ireland, grew up in Canada and lives in London.